THE ESSENTIALS

Supporting Dual Language Learners

in Diverse Environments in Preschool & Kindergarten

Iliana Alanís, María G. Arreguín, & Irasema Salinas-González

National Association for the Education of Young Children
Washington, DC

National Association for the
Education of Young Children
1401 H Street, NW, Suite 600
Washington, DC 20005
202-232-8777 • 800-424-2460
NAEYC.org

NAEYC Books

Senior Director, Publishing
& Content Development
Susan Friedman

Director, Books
Dana Battaglia

Senior Editor
Holly Bohart

Editor
Rossella Procopio

Senior Creative Design Manager
Henrique J. Siblesz

Senior Creative Design Specialist
Charity Coleman

Senior Creative Design Specialist
Gillian Frank

Publishing Business
Operations Manager
Francine Markowitz

Permissions

NAEYC provides requests for limited use of our copyrighted material. For permission to reprint, adapt, translate, or otherwise reuse and repurpose content from this publication, review our guidelines at NAEYC.org/resources/permissions.

Photo Credits

Photos on pages iv, 1, 33 © Getty Images.

All other photographs courtesy of the authors.

The Essentials: Supporting Dual Language Learners in Diverse Environments in Preschool & Kindergarten. Copyright © 2021 by the National Association for the Education of Young Children. All rights reserved. Printed in the United States of America.

Library of Congress Control Number: 2020937678

ISBN: 978-1-938113-81-9

Item: 1151

Contents

Acknowledgments

We want to acknowledge those who contributed to this book in large and small ways. First, we thank Susan Friedman, senior director of publishing and professional learning at NAEYC, for bringing us this important work and assisting us along the way. We also acknowledge NAEYC's efforts and commitment to provide developmentally, culturally, and linguistically appropriate instruction and assessment for dual language learners across the United States.

We thank Dr. Socorro García-Alvarado, Dr. Raquel Cataldo, Dr. Mariandrea Pérez, Ms. Erika López Playle, Mrs. Arlen García, and Mr. Michael Larralde, who lent their expertise by reading and commenting on various chapters. A special thank-you to Dr. Leo Gómez whose leading work in dual language education for the last 25 years has impacted the lives of children and the families they represent.

We are extremely grateful for the many early childhood educators who have opened their doors and allowed us into their classrooms to implement lessons, take photos, and learn from their children. *¡Gracias por su ejemplo!* Your work inspires and motivates us!

Lastly, we recognize our families who continue to support and encourage our work.

About the Book

While the early childhood profession has a strong understanding of developmentally appropriate practice for children from birth through age 8 (Copple & Bredekamp 2009), there is less certainty about educating young emergent bilingual children, also known as *dual language learners* (DLLs). Educators, for example, may be unsure as to what language to use for instruction, how to develop biliteracy, or how to provide input that is comprehensible. They may be unclear as to what language families should be using at home when children are receiving English instruction at school, or how to engage with non-English-speaking families. What is clear, however, is that access to quality education for young DLLs is critical in order to attain academic success. The challenges of learning in English-only classrooms, and the persistent schooling inequalities experienced by DLLs and their families, reaffirm the urgency.

DLLs benefit from highly qualified and reflective teachers who provide culturally, linguistically, and developmentally appropriate experiences and interactions in curricula and instruction (NASEM 2017). The National Association for the Education of Young Children's (NAEYC's) position statement "Advancing Equity in Early Childhood Education" (2019) reminds us of our ethical responsibility to create a society where all children thrive. This effort will require systemic changes and educators who continuously reflect on their practice as they develop an understanding of the sociocultural process of learning in two (or more) languages, as well as the ramifications of inequitable schooling for DLLs and their families.

Research is clear—the most effective schooling for young DLLs, including DLLs with disabilities, is a bilingual program with a certified bilingual teacher who provides instruction in a child's home language and English (Genesee & Fortune 2014; NASEM 2017; Thomas & Collier 2012). However, it is challenging to find certified bilingual teachers for every language group (Arias & Markos 2016). Thus, many educational programs have implemented English-as-a-second-language (ESL) programs with certified ESL teachers who are trained in developing academic content using second-language acquisition practices (e.g., visuals, body languages, realia). Unfortunately, bilingual and ESL programs may not be available for all dual language learners. Thus, all teachers need to understand how bilingualism influences linguistic, cognitive, and socioemotional development. Our intent with this text is to provide essential and practical information to support teachers of preschool and kindergarten children attending group settings or classrooms where they are learning English as a second or third language.

Who Is This Book For?

This book is for early childhood educators who work or will work with the growing number of DLLs within the age range of 3 to 5 in family home centers, private preschool centers, Head Start classrooms, or state-funded preschool and kindergarten programs. General education teachers, bilingual teachers, ESL teachers, and special education therapists will find the information useful. Instructional leaders, such as program directors and administrators, who work with children in preschool and kindergarten will also find the information beneficial as they develop partnerships with families and colleagues.

Why This Book?

We wrote this text with this question in mind: What do early childhood educators need to understand to better address the linguistic, cognitive, and socioemotional needs of all DLLs in their classrooms? We each bring over two decades of experience working with Spanish- and English-speaking populations in bilingual settings as bilingual teachers, university professors, researchers, and professional development providers. The majority of the teachers we work with are in dual language programs with Spanish- and English-dominant speakers learning academic content in two languages. It is through this lens that we approached the writing of this text.

There are over 350 languages spoken within the United States (US Census Bureau 2015). This means emergent bilingual children come from a variety of cultural and linguistic backgrounds. We acknowledge that it is impossible for a teacher to teach in all languages. All teachers, however, can gain a richer understanding of the interdependent relationship among culture, language, and learning. With this understanding, teachers can implement intentional practices that nurture children's bilingual identities and augment their growth in all developmental domains. Educators can apply the concepts and strategies we present in a variety of early childhood settings and contexts.

What Is in This Book?

Using current and foundational research, we provide developmentally and linguistically appropriate guidance for intentional and purposeful practices with children, their families, and other members of the school community. Children are shaped by the social, cultural, and historical contexts in which they live (Vygotsky 1978). To that end, in Part 1 of the text we provide an overview of the defining characteristics of DLLs, specifically outlining the demographic, historical, and policy factors that have influenced current conversations in the field of bilingual education. We focus on the intricate connections between family and culture to better understand the complexities embedded in young children's bilingual and bicultural trajectories both at home and in their formal education settings.

Chapter 1 describes the various labels used for DLLs and provides an overview of dual language learner demographics in the United States. This context is important because it highlights the urgency of this work. We discuss the significance of getting to know the backgrounds, previous experiences, cultures, and linguistic resources for the families in your setting. We include information on how to engage with families of cultural and linguistic diversity.

Chapter 2 describes the differences between sequential and simultaneous bilinguals. We focus on the vocabulary development of DLLs and the idea that exposure and active involvement in meaningful activities will accelerate vocabulary building and will enhance children's ability to participate in increasingly complex conversations and language production. We provide strategies for vocabulary development that require teachers to focus on meaning and open up cross-language spaces where children can apply what they know and transfer concepts from one language to another.

Chapter 3 provides considerations for educators who are investigating the implementation of a dual language program. We identify goals of dual language programs and describe options for allocating the home and English language throughout the school day. We discuss the significance of language input that is representational, interactional, and imaginative for children's overall development. We conclude with a description of the crucial differences between language of instruction, language of learning, and language of communication as we emphasize the need to prioritize the cognitive engagement of DLLs.

Part 2 of the text focuses on how educators can create culturally and linguistically appropriate experiences and instruction for children in bilingual and English-medium classrooms.

In Chapter 4, we focus on carefully planned environments for DLLs that support their learning and development while valuing their language and culture. We describe the use of print resources such as labels, signs, word walls, and child-created alphabets. We identify materials and spaces that support DLLs in the classroom and essential supports such as schedules, routines, and transitions. Finally, we provide information regarding inclusive learning environments for DLLs.

In Chapter 5, we focus on creating culturally relevant play spaces where playful learning activities become opportunities to scaffold language as children use their full language potential in translingual play. We determine the role of the teacher as a language guide and discuss how play also supports the development of DLLs with disabilities.

In Chapter 6, we move our discussion to the significance of integrating all language skills in the development of biliteracy. We propose and describe an interdisciplinary inquiry approach for biliteracy development that teachers can use across the content areas and highlight strategies that promote biliteracy development for DLLs in dual language classrooms.

In Chapter 7, we focus on children in English-medium classrooms with a range of languages and children in dual language programs who will also receive English instruction. We provide developmentally, culturally, and linguistically appropriate strategies that teachers can apply within multiple contexts but that are critical when working with DLLs. We use examples from two classrooms to identify multimodal teaching, culturally authentic literacy-related activities, and partner-based strategies that strengthen and support children's overall development.

In Chapter 8, we focus on authentic assessment practices and emphasize the need to develop reciprocal relationships with children's families throughout the assessment process. We describe the unique aspects of bilingualism that contribute to children's learning and development, something that is often misunderstood in the assessment process. We concentrate on the use of authentic assessments that capture emergent bilingual children's strengths and needs. We highlight data documentation and collection through anecdotal notes, observations, photos, audio, and video recordings.

Finally, in Chapter 9, we peek into Ms. Rocha's Spanish–English dual language prekindergarten classroom as she engages DLLs in specific moments of her day. We describe the strategies she uses to activate children's previous knowledge and augment children's English vocabulary using their listening, speaking, reading, and writing abilities. We highlight how she engages children through comprehensible input and active learning as she develops science concepts and emergent literacy. We also follow Ms. Rocha as she observes and informally assesses children in learning centers. We note how she intentionally plans play-based learning activities that support children's linguistic, socioemotional, and academic development.

Text Features

We use each chapter to introduce a concept from a developmental and asset-based perspective that focuses on the role of a child's home language and their family in the educational process. Using current research, we frame what the reader needs to know about each concept. When appropriate, we integrate how teachers can support DLLs with disabilities.

Each chapter opens with a vignette that exemplifies children's and teacher's experiences within an educational context. Where appropriate, we provide strategies teachers can use around each concept using an Idea Box that provides practical ways for educators to apply their understanding in practice. Additionally, we provide definitions of specialized or significant vocabulary. We conclude each chapter with Key Points to Remember, Frequently Asked Questions, and Connections to NAEYC Accreditation Program Standards. At the end of the book, we provide additional resources for more information and guidance.

We have also created a sample syllabus and sample activities that connect to each chapter. These can be found online at **NAEYC.org/essentials-supporting-DLLs**.

References

Arias, M.B., & A.M. Markos. 2016. *Characteristics of the Workforce Who Are Educating and Supporting Children Who Are English Language Learners*. Unpublished manuscript commissioned by the Committee on Fostering School Success for English.

Copple, C., & S. Bredekamp, eds. 2009. *Developmentally Appropriate Practice in Early Childhood Programs from Birth Through Age 8*. 3rd ed. Washington, DC: NAEYC.

Genesee, F., & T. Fortune. 2014. "Bilingual Education and At-Risk Students." *Journal of Immersion and Content-Based Language Education* 2 (2): 196–209.

NAEYC. 2019. "Advancing Equity in Early Childhood Education." Position statement. Washington, DC: NAEYC. www.naeyc.org /resources/position-statements/equity.

NASEM (National Academies of Sciences, Engineering, and Medicine). 2017. *Promoting the Educational Success of Children and Youth Learning English: Promising Futures*. Washington, DC: National Academies Press. doi:10.17226/24677.

Thomas, W.P., & V.P. Collier. 2012. *Dual Language Education for a Transformed World*. Albuquerque, NM: Fuente Press.

US Census Bureau. 2015. "Census Bureau Reports at Least 350 Languages Spoken in U.S. Homes." www.census.gov/newsroom/press -releases/2015/cb15-185.html.

Vygotsky, L. 1978. *Mind in Society: The Development of Higher Psychological Processes*. Cambridge, MA: Harvard University Press.

Understanding the Essentials

Start speak Spanish at home; however, Head Start children and their families speak more than 140 languages.

Getting to Know DLLs in Your Context

Dual language learners' patterns of continuous growth reveal the urgency in adopting initiatives, curricula, and pedagogy that effectively serve their academic, linguistic, and socioemotional needs. This necessitates that educators understand and address the needs of DLLs within their local contexts. In this section, we move to the need to gather information about the children and their families within your center or school.

An initial conversation with families will help you establish meaningful partnerships that will lead to children's overall success. Families are experts when it comes to their children and their development (Copple & Bredekamp 2009). As such, learn what is appropriate in each child's family and community (Souto-Manning 2013). Learning about the social, linguistic, and cultural backgrounds of the children at your center or school helps you understand who they are and where they come from. This understanding is crucial to provide effective support for their learning and development.

To meet families' needs, it will also be helpful if you know the families at your center or school. For example, did families move into your community because a family member is attending a local university? Alternatively, are families moving into your area to find employment? Or seeking political asylum? It is helpful to know who cares for the child. As of the writing of this book, the United States has experienced an increase in unaccompanied minors and/or children separated from their families at the border; therefore, some children in your center may not be living with their biological parents but with extended family members or caregivers (Dreby 2015). Schools are also seeing an increase in refugee families who have experienced conflict and trauma. This trend will likely continue. What resources do the families of the children you teach need to adjust to their new community? Answers to these questions can inform decisions in terms of instruction, family involvement, and school-wide initiatives.

> ## What If You Do Not Speak the Family's Language?
>
> › Hire bilingual staff members who can serve as interpreters.
>
> › Cultivate the linguistic wealth of your community; find members of the community who speak the family's language.
>
> › Invite current family members to speak with new families.
>
> › Hire translators and/or bilingual staff to support families with the enrollment and screening process.
>
> › Contact your local college or university's bilingual education or foreign language education department to hire translators and/or interpreters.

While it is recommended to learn more about each family's background and context, it is not appropriate to ask about a family's immigration status. All children have the right to a public education regardless of citizenship or residency status, as indicated in the 1982 *Plyler v. Doe* US Supreme Court case. Review your current registration forms and requirements for unnecessary questions (e.g., it is not necessary to ask for a child's social security number). Read questions on enrollment forms from a family's perspective, and be respectful of their decision not to provide information.

Plyler v. Doe
US Supreme Court case that indicates that states cannot constitutionally deny children a free public education because of their immigration status (American Immigration Council 2016).

What Languages Do Your DLLs Speak?

As indicated earlier, DLLs represent a variety of language groups. To gain a better understanding of children's linguistic assets and how to meet their linguistic needs, inquire about the language(s) spoken at home and by whom. Some children from Guatemala and Mexico, for example, may speak indigenous languages such as Mayan or Mixtec—sometimes in addition to Spanish—and are also learning a third language (English) at school (Kovats Sánchez 2018). As more immigrant children arrive at your school or center, it will be necessary to determine the multiple languages children may be proficient in within their home context (see Language Inventory in Chapter 6 and Home Language Survey in Chapter 8). Regardless of where children are from or what languages they speak, all children have the right to receive high-quality instruction in an environment that values and embraces their linguistic and cultural assets.

Strategies to Develop Relationships with DLLs and Their Families in Your Context

Given the changing demographics, it is crucial for teachers to create culturally and linguistically responsive environments that incorporate families' cultural and linguistic resources. There are multiple considerations when creating opportunities to engage families in children's learning and development. Begin with simple but relevant steps that will help you develop and nurture reciprocal relationships with families.

Create a Welcoming and Respectful Environment

High-quality programs create a welcoming environment (Copple & Bredekamp 2009) that reflects families' communication tools, resources, and personal connection. The environment within the common areas of your center or school and individual classrooms should affirm families' languages. Large banners or signs that read "Welcome to our school" in multiple languages, for example, display respect for various languages. Provide the necessary supports to your front office staff who are often the first representatives of a program to interact with families. Bilingual staff will help families feel reassured that their presence and diversity are valued. These might also include translated documents, access to interpreters, or community resources. Keep in mind, it is not appropriate to ask children to translate for their families. This creates an uncomfortable situation between families and children and can damage their relationships (Adair & Barraza 2019).

Use a variety of formal and informal means (e.g., emails, phone calls, home visits) to reach out and welcome families into your center or school community. Consider the significance of making this outreach personal and face-to-face. Ask families about their preferred means of communication. Once the school year begins, texting families can be an effective method to maintain communication (Loeb & York 2016). Helping families feel welcomed and respected will build positive relationships that lead to long-term positive student outcomes (Martinez-Hickman & Amaro-Jiménez 2018).

Validate Children's Languages and Identities

To demonstrate support and respect for bilingual families, attempt to learn some of the home languages of the children you teach. Families appreciate when teachers learn basic phrases like "Hello, how are you?" and "Thank you" (Adair & Barraza 2019). Ask family members for additional phrases, greetings, and conversation starters such as "Happy birthday" or "Good morning." Incorporate these words into your classroom routines so that all children learn about other languages (Baker & Páez 2018). This will also help children adjust to their new surroundings and strengthen relationships with families.

Make a concerted effort to value children's identities by learning the correct pronunciation of their names, including families' surnames, and avoid giving children different names that are easier to pronounce. Extend this idea into your classroom and ensure that all children learn to pronounce their classmates' names (Warsi 2017). When we pronounce names correctly, individuals feel validated and respected, which is crucial for psychological and educational outcomes. (Visit www.mynamemyidentity.org for more information.)

Acknowledge Anxiety

All children and families come into a new situation with some apprehension. Many bilingual families come into your center or school with the additional challenges of not understanding the language, lack of familiarity with the US schooling system, and not knowing the teacher's expectations. It is important for you to listen and respond to families' questions or concerns. They may question how their child will learn the primary language of the school or wonder what language they should be speaking at home. They may worry or have concerns about how their child will learn to read in another language. Help families feel at ease and comfortable with their decision to place their children in your care and reassure them that their children are in a safe environment. Ask families how to best comfort their children and do not hesitate to show affection to express your care for children (Adair & Barraza 2019).

Recognize Diversity in Family Involvement

Families who did not attend school in the United States may not be aware of expectations for family involvement in US classrooms or in your specific setting (Martinez-Hickman & Amaro-Jiménez 2018). Some families may be willing to volunteer and share their expertise, but others may believe getting their children to school on time and ready to learn is how they contribute to their child's education. Zárate (2007) found that "Latino parents believed that monitoring their children's lives and providing moral guidance resulted in good classroom behavior, which in turn allowed for greater academic learning opportunities" (9). In Zárate's study, families identified "moral guidance" as parental involvement. Embrace nontraditional contributions.

Invite families to contribute their time and knowledge (Baker & Páez 2018). Realize that family backgrounds may influence their desire to spend time on a campus or center. For example, immigration policies and threats of deportation raids may negatively influence family involvement (Gándara & Ee 2018). Supporting a family's decisions as to how they engage in family involvement is an essential aspect to developing respectful home–school partnerships.

Share Information with Families

It is important for you to provide families with information about their children's education. This might include

> The goals of the bilingual, ESL, or general education program

> How you will support the development of the child's first language as she gains proficiency in English

> How families can support what you are doing at school

> How you will support what families are already doing at home to help children develop language, literacy, and numeracy skills

This information should be meaningful, easy to understand, and specific (see "Additional Resources" for guidance).

Invite families to spend some time in their children's classroom. This way they can learn more about your classroom routines and your approach to instruction. These visits allow family members to share their home literacy practices. They can also experience how their children are learning

Using Your Environment to Support Multiple Languages

> Along the hallways, main office, library, and cafeteria, post signage that includes both visual symbols and text that represents the multiple languages within your educational context.

> Have children greet each other using the multiple languages represented in your context.

> Discuss the need to purchase books in children's home language with your school librarian.

Addressing Families' Fears and Anxieties

> Reassure families that activities such as reading, talking, and singing with children in their home language will promote biliteracy development by establishing a strong linguistic foundation in their home language.

> Provide families with information about the time needed to develop a second or third language.

> Recognize families' cultural and linguistic expertise by asking them questions and inviting them to share cultural activities or knowledge.

> Approach the teacher–family dialogue as a way to support your own professional learning (Isik-Ercan, forthcoming).

and observe how they engage with peers. Encourage family members to ask questions and offer their suggestions to make the learning environment more welcoming and effective for their child.

Recognize Family's Rights

As indicated earlier, all children have the right to a public education in the United States. This includes access to bilingual education programs and special education services. Early childhood educators have a responsibility to ensure children receive the instruction and support services needed to be successful (NAEYC 2016). Families should receive information about programs, services, and school policies in their home language and in terms they can understand so they can advocate for their children's needs. Whenever possible, provide a family liaison or advocate who can be the bridge between the child's home and the school.

Summary

Language, culture, and identity are interrelated. Understanding the multidimensional lives of DLLs and their families will help you create a culturally and linguistically supportive environment for children's learning and development. Supporting families involves the development of reciprocal and respectful relationships that help families and children feel validated and accepted. Involving families in their child's learning and development will lead to positive outcomes for children, families, and educators.

Key Points to Remember!

> Learning about the social, linguistic, and cultural backgrounds of the children at your center or school helps you understand who they are and where they come from.

> While it is recommended to learn more about each family's background and context, it is not appropriate to ask about a family's immigration status.

> It is not appropriate to ask children to translate for their families. This creates an uncomfortable situation between families and children and can damage their relationships (Adair & Barraza 2019).

> Invite families to spend some time in their children's classroom. This way they can learn more about your classroom routines and your approach to instruction.

Frequently Asked Questions

What language should families speak at home?

Often, bilingual families are unsure if they should continue to speak their native language at home or if they should speak to their child in English. Bilingual families recognize the power of English in this country. After all, to be successful within the United States, one must command the English language. Families, therefore, want their children to learn English. According to a report by NASEM (2017), however, "DLLs who fail to maintain proficiency in their home language may lose their ability to communicate with parents and family members and may risk becoming estranged from their cultural and linguistic heritage" (6). Families should continue to build their children's home languages through storytelling, book sharing, songs, and child-directed conversations (Espinosa 2013).

How can I support a child's home language in the classroom?

The development of a strong foundation in a child's home language will support development of their second or third language. Even when the language of instruction is English, teachers should continue to develop the child's home language through labels in the classroom, songs, and learning some words and phrases in the child's home language.

References

Adair, J.K., & A. Barraza. 2019. "Voice of Immigrant Families in Early Childhood Settings." In *Spotlight on Young Children: Equity and Diversity,* eds. C. Gillanders & R. Procopio, 34–54. Washington, DC: NAEYC.

American Immigration Council. 2016. "Public Education for Immigrant Students: Understanding Plyler v. Doe," October 24. www.americanimmigrationcouncil.org /research/plyler-v-doe-public-education -immigrant-students.

Baker, M., & M. Páez. 2018. *The Language of the Classroom: Dual Language Learners in Head Start, Public PreK, and Private Preschool Programs.* Washington, DC: Migration Policy Institute.

Capps, R. 2015. *Trends in Immigration and Migration of English and Dual Language Learners.* Presented to the National Research Council Committee on Fostering School Success for English Learners, Washington, DC, May 28.

Copple, C., & S. Bredekamp, eds. 2009. *Developmentally Appropriate Practice in Early Childhood Programs from Birth Through Age 8.* 3rd ed. Washington, DC: NAEYC.

Crosnoe, R., & R.N. López-Turley. 2011. "K–12 Educational Outcomes of Immigrant Youth." *Future of Children* 21 (1): 129–52.

Dreby, J. 2015. "U.S. Immigration Policy and Family Separation: The Consequences for Children's Well-Being." *Social Science & Medicine* 132: 245–251.

Espinosa, L. 2013. *Early Education for Dual Language Learners: Promoting School Readiness and Early School Success.* Washington, DC: Migration Policy Institute.

Gándara, P., & J. Ee. 2018. *Working Paper: US Immigration Enforcement Policy and Its Impact on Teaching and Learning in the Nation's Schools.* The Civil Rights Project, UCLA. www.civilrightsproject.ucla.edu /research/k-12-education/immigration -immigrant-students/u.s.-immigration -enforcement-policy-and-its-impact-on -teaching-and-learning-in-the-nations-schools.

García, O., & J.A. Kleifgen. 2010. *Educating Emergent Bilinguals: Policies, Programs, and Practices for English Language Learners.* New York: Teachers College Press.

García, O., J.A. Kleifgen, & L. Falchi. 2008. *Equity Perspectives: From English Language Learners to Emergent Bilinguals. Campaign for Educational Equity*: New York: Teachers College, Columbia University.

Garcia, O., & T. Kleyn. 2016. *Translanguaging with Multilingual Students: Learning from Classroom Moments.* New York: Routledge.

González-Barrera, A., & M.H. López. 2013. *Spanish Is the Most Spoken Non-English Language in US Homes, Even Among Hispanics.* Washington, DC: Pew Research Center.

Isik-Ercan, Z. Forthcoming. "Developing the 3 Cs of Reciprocity." In *Advancing Equity in Early Childhood Education,* eds. I. Alanís & I.U. Iruka, with B. Willer & S. Friedman. Washington, DC: NAEYC.

Kovats Sánchez, G. 2018. "Reaffirming Indigenous Identity: Understanding Experiences of Stigmatization and Marginalization Among Mexican Indigenous College Students." *Journal of Latinos in Education.* doi:10.1080/15348431.2018.1447484.

Lee, J., & M. Zhou. 2015. *The Asian American Achievement Paradox.* New York: Russell Sage Foundation.

Loeb, S., & B. York. 2016. "Helping Parents Help Their Children." Brookings. www.brookings.edu/research/helping-parents-help-their-children.

Martinez-Hickman, O., & C. Amaro-Jiménez. 2018. "When Parents Get Involved, Things Just Get Better. Lessons from Latino/a Parents' Experiences in Public Schools." *NABE Perspectives* 41 (2).

NAEYC. 2016. *Code of Ethical Conduct and Statement of Commitment.* Brochure. Rev. ed. Washington, DC: NAEYC.

NASEM (National Academies of Sciences, Engineering, and Medicine). 2017. *Promoting the Educational Success of Children and Youth Learning English: Promising Futures.* Washington, DC: National Academies Press. doi:10.17226/24677.

NCELA (National Clearinghouse on English Language Acquisition). 2018. "Fact Sheets." https://ncela.ed.gov/fast-facts.

Office of Head Start. 2008. National Head Start Act. https://eclkc.ohs.acf.hhs.gov/policy/head-start-act

Souto-Manning, M. 2013. "Preschool Through Primary Grades: Teaching Young Children from Immigrant and Diverse Families." *Young Children* 68 (4): 72–81.

US Department of Health and Human Services, Administration for Children and Families, Office of Head Start. 2018. "Head Start Program Facts: Fiscal Year 2018." https://eclkc.ohs.acf.hhs.gov/about-us/article/head-start-program-facts-fiscal-year-2018.

Warsi, S. 2017. "Welcoming Refugee Children into Early Childhood Classrooms." *Teaching Young Children* 10 (5): 12–15.

Zárate, M.E. 2007. *Understanding Latino Parent Involvement in Education: Perceptions, Expectations, and Recommendations.* Los Angeles: Tomás Rivera Policy Institute.

naeyc® Accreditation
Early Learning Programs

This chapter supports the following NAEYC Early Learning Program Accreditation Standards and Topic Areas:

Standard 1: Relationships
1.A Building Positive Relationships Between Teachers and Families

Standard 7: Families
7.A Knowing and Understanding the Program's Families

7.B Sharing Information Between Staff and Families

7.C Nurturing Families as Advocates for Their Children

2 What Does It Mean to Develop Two Languages?

Objectives

> Distinguish between sequential and simultaneous bilingualism.

> Identify how dual language learners display their languages in a dual language classroom.

> Discuss vocabulary development in dual language learners.

> Describe strategies for children developing two languages.

Sheila has noticed that more children in her Head Start classroom speak languages other than English. This year, Sheila is particularly concerned because two children, Carla and Samuel, speak Mixteco, a language she has not encountered before. While the other five dual language learners in her classroom speak Spanish and Sheila is somewhat proficient in that language, she now wonders how to better address the cognitive, socioemotional, and language needs of all the children she teaches.

Ensuring that dual language learners (DLLs) encounter opportunities to reach their full potential in formal and informal educational settings is a goal that involves careful planning and close collaboration between families and educators. Although formal dual language programs are not always feasible in our classrooms, as educators, it is necessary to integrate developmentally appropriate practices that target the needs of children who are culturally and linguistically diverse. We are also challenged to adopt responsive pedagogies and research-evidenced practices to promote academic excellence.

As you recall from Chapter 1, a dual language learner is a child developing two languages at the same time. However, DLLs develop bilingualism in diverse contexts. A *simultaneous bilingual* child may be found in households where family members are bilingual or where one family member speaks a different language, allowing for consistent exposure to meaningful communication in both languages, generally before the age of 3. A *sequential bilingual,* on the other hand, is a child who initially acquires a first language at home and often begins school or formal education in a setting where a different language is used as a medium of instruction. Knowing the difference between sequential and simultaneous bilingual children is important because the linguistic support needed will vary considerably (as will be discussed in upcoming chapters).

Despite concerns regarding children's ability to develop two languages at a young age, all children can be educated bilingually without negative effects (NASEM 2017). We also know that although the oral language of DLLs may reflect elements of two or more languages, this does not mean that these children are confusing the different languages. In fact, they closely mirror patterns of development that we observe in monolingual children (e.g., receptive language skills develop before expressive language skills). Work by García and Wei (2014) has led to our understanding that bilingualism of DLLs is dynamic. As bilingualism develops, children will learn to separate their two languages based on who the audience is and the type of task they are performing.

How Do DLLs Display Their Languages in an Early Childhood Classroom?

Because the language practices of DLLs are complex and dynamic, identifying their most dominant language may not be easy. We know that any given classroom may include emergent bilinguals whose family members fall in varied categories. Here are just some examples of the multitude of ways a child in a two-parent household might experience bilingualism:

> Mother speaks only English and father speaks only Spanish.

> Father speaks only Spanish and mother speaks only English.

> Father and mother are bilingual (English and Spanish or other language).

> Mother speaks a language other than English or Spanish (e.g., Mixteco, Russian, French) while father speaks only English.

> Both parents speak only Spanish or another language other than English.

> Both parents speak English and other caregivers speak Spanish or another language.

> Family members speak three or more languages.

> Tutors (caregivers) and parents speak three different languages.

One or a combination of these scenarios is likely to apply to many DLLs present in your classroom. It is important to keep in mind that, in many cases, young children interact for significant amounts of time with a monolingual individual who strongly influences the language environment and the type of activities the child engages in. Grandparents or a close relative, for example, may be the primary caregivers and important language models for the young child. How adults interact with children impacts their academic, linguistic, and social development (Dombro, Jablon, & Stetson 2020). Vocabulary and grammatical growth, for instance, correlates with the quality and quantity of speech that bilingual children hear in each language (Ramírez-Esparza, García-Sierra, & Kuhl 2016). Quality features of language can be measured in terms of the extent to which adults use "different word types and the different ideas conveyed by those words" (NASEM 2017, 131).

How to Incorporate Discussions of Language and Culture

> Plan conversations that encourage children to share the different languages they use in their social circles (e.g., "Tell your partner about the language you use with your grandmother; tell us about the things you do with your family").

> Share stories about your own exposure to different languages and cultures. This will convey the message that diversity is important and is valued.

Do All DLLs Become Proficient Balanced Bilinguals?

Balanced bilinguals are individuals whose proficiency in two languages closely resembles the communicative skills of a native speaker. Operating with ease in most social and academic settings is an achievable goal when support is systematically embedded in the educational system. Unfortunately, not all DLLs become balanced bilinguals.

DLLs follow diverse language paths as they begin their formal educational experience. Although oversimplified, Figure 2.1 shows that when bilingual children begin formal education, they can either be in settings that augment or subtract from their linguistic skills. In **subtractive language environments**, DLLs can lose their first language or key language skills to a significant degree, resulting in limited bilingualism. Subtractive settings can be found in homes or classrooms that intentionally or unintentionally favor one language while minimizing exposure to the other language. **Additive language environments**, on the other hand, are settings in which adults promote children's entire range of language skills. They foster a bilingual identity and thus develop a child's bilingualism.

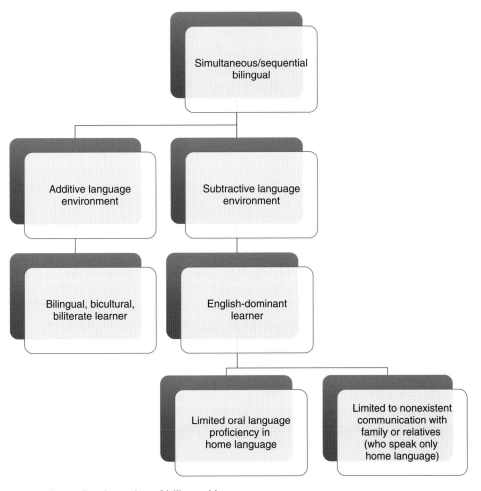

Figure 2.1. Bilingual trajectories of bilingual learners.

Vocabulary Development in DLLs: How Is It Different?

subtractive language environments
Environments where DLLs have few opportunities to speak, listen, read, and write in their home language. In these settings, English is the predominant language of instruction and the language reflected in most instructional materials and environmental print.

additive language environments
Environments where DLLs have many opportunities to speak, listen, read, and write in their home language and in English.

schema
The mental ability of DLLs to make sense of their experiences and guide their behavior.

We know that for DLLs, a key predictor of academic success is the amount of quality language experience children receive in their home language (Collier & Thomas 2009). These experiences involve the use of rich vocabulary and varied types of sentences in relation to objects or actions that interest children. A crucial aspect behind this principle is the idea that exposure and active involvement in meaningful activities will accelerate vocabulary building and will enhance the ability to participate in increasingly complex conversations and language production.

To better understand how DLLs build vocabulary, it is important to discuss two key ideas: (1) multiple labels (or terms) are acquired for objects, concepts, and events, and (2) knowledge learned in one language will transfer to any other language the child acquires.

Children develop vocabulary or their semantic knowledge in formal and informal contexts. Their experiences lead to labels for objects, events, concepts, and object-label associations (**schema**). Given their characteristics and pattern of language development (exposure to multiple language contexts), DLLs develop flexibility with languages that allows them to accept and expect multiple labels for the same object, event, or concept (NASEM 2017).

Understanding how DLLs develop vocabulary is crucial to the design of experiences that enhance their semantic knowledge. It also allows educators to properly assess vocabulary size and growth (see Chapter 8). To illustrate this point, let's look at how Gabriela, a 4-year-old DLL, has developed a sophisticated vocabulary across both Spanish and English:

> Gabriela is a simultaneous DLL who was born in Texas. She enjoys the outdoors and can often be found playing with rocks, twigs, and other treasures that she discovers. Gabriela's parents are bilingual speakers but predominately use English at home with some occasional Spanish. On the weekends, Gabriela enjoys watching sports activities with her father and accompanying him to basketball games, where she often pretends to participate in the activities from the sidelines while playing with other children. At bedtime, her parents read English-language books. During the week, her maternal grandparents, who are monolingual Spanish speakers, pick her up from school and spend the afternoon helping her with homework and cooking the family's dinner. They also devote some time to their beekeeping. On Wednesdays and Sundays, Gabriela and her family attend a religious mass, delivered in Spanish.

Gabriela's vocabulary knowledge has partially come from her experiences, which have allowed her to accumulate a significant number of labels in each language. However, Table 2.1 shows that when considered in isolation, Gabriela's vocabulary in English gives only a partial picture of her semantic knowledge.

Although Gabriela may initially have been exposed to the words *reina* and *obrera* only in Spanish, she will learn and accept the words *queen* and *worker bee* without hesitation. This is because the adults in her life will also use these words interchangeably. The fact that labels are arbitrary is what provides DLLs with **metalinguistic awareness** (Bialystok 2015). Eventually Gabriela will acquire vocabulary across both languages, or a vast **linguistic repertoire** (García & Wei 2014; MacSwan 2017).

metalinguistic awareness
The process of analyzing our own language processes.

linguistic repertoire
This refers to DLLs using all of their full language capabilities to communicate and make meaning.

Over time, the vocabulary development of DLLs will follow a progression, as shown here:

1. Labels learned in one language (e.g., Spanish) will be associated with concepts initially acquired in another language (e.g., English); for example, when Gabriela learns that another name for *team* is *equipo*.

2. Labels initially acquired in one language (e.g., English) will eventually be transferred to the second or third language (e.g., Spanish). For example, a child may learn that the concept of *buoyancy* in English translates into *flotabilidad* in Spanish.

Table 2.1. A Glimpse of Gabriela's Linguistic Repertoire

Sample Vocabulary Gabriela Initially Acquired Only in English while Playing Golf and Watching Basketball Games with Her Father	Sample Vocabulary Gabriela Acquired Mainly in Spanish while Engaging in Activities with Her Spanish-Speaking Maternal Grandparents
airball	*enjambre* (swarm)
backswing	*reina* (queen)
backspin	*obrera* (worker bee)
birdie	*zángano* (drone)
basket	*cera* (wax)
caddie	*vela* (candle)
coach	*Molcajete* (mortar)
foul	*manzanilla* (chamomile)
penalty	*masa* (dough)
shank	*confesión* (confession)
score	*iglesia* (church)
team	*padre* (priest)
Spurs	*especias* (spices)
	tarea (homework)

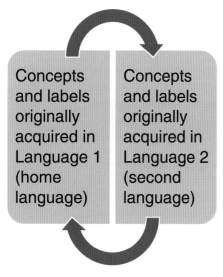

Figure 2.2. The concept of language transfer plays a key role in vocabulary growth for DLLs (Cummins 2000).

DLLs will seamlessly navigate two language contexts with ease in both directions (English ↔ Spanish) using appropriate or expected languages depending on a given situation. Knowledge can be learned, expressed, and transferred from and to any language, as shown in Figure 2.2.

Strategies for Developing Two Languages

When designing instruction for DLLs, keep in mind that these children deserve the same high-quality education as their English-speaking peers so they can achieve developmentally appropriate objectives. This means providing challenging and engaging experiences purposefully designed to capitalize on DLLs linguistic diversity, ensuring that the language learned in their homes is used as an asset as they embark on a bilingual or multilingual path.

All early childhood educators, including families, can significantly impact children's language development by being responsive and interacting purposefully (Otto 2018). Whether instruction is delivered in English or in the child's home language, DLLs thrive linguistically when teachers focus on meaning and open up cross-language spaces where children can transfer what they know in one language to another.

Focus on Meaning

As simultaneous and sequential bilingual children engage in verbal and nonverbal behaviors, they primarily focus on meaning. In other words, children seldom pay attention to language correctness. In order to maintain focus on the significance of an event or object, it is critical that adults also prioritize children's meaning-making efforts. Let's look at an example:

> As part of her science lesson, Ms. Young has created an opportunity for her 3-year-old students to play with objects in water. Mario picks up a twig and throws it into a bucket of water. He notices the twig floats.
>
> He excitedly shouts, "Look, *adiba*!" (Look on top!)
>
> Ms. Young responds, "Yes! You noticed how the twig floats in the water. What else did you observe?"

Ms. Young focused on what Mario discovered—qualities of water in a sink or float scenario. Instead of emphasizing a lack of language correctness, she capitalized on the opportunity to validate what Mario said and augment his English vocabulary.

You may have noticed that Mario codeswitched—that is, he used both English and Spanish: *Look* (in English) and *adiba* (his pronunciation of *arriba* in Spanish). In addition to focusing on meaning, Ms. Young used vocabulary that was relevant to Mario's immediate interest. The words *twig, float,* and *observe* connected with Mario's actions and made vocabulary acquisition natural and pleasurable.

Cross-Language Spaces

Along with a focus on meaning, early childhood educators can facilitate a child's understanding by establishing cross-language opportunities. These "purposefully planned opportunities to compare languages" allow DLLs to transfer and build proficiency in both languages (Escamilla et al. 2014, 68). For example, in the morning, teachers can play games such as "Read the Room" in Spanish on Mondays, Wednesdays, and Fridays. In doing so, they review names of items in the classroom, adjectives that apply to those items, and other grammatical components. Then on Tuesday and Thursday, the same routine is followed in English. This will encourage children to compare the languages they use.

Providing opportunities to compare languages does not need to involve direct or concurrent translation. Purposeful planning involves designating specific times, activities, and routines that spark conversations related to how languages are alike and how they are different. Teachers in dual language classrooms sometimes implement rhymes and guessing games in the morning routine. A dual language classroom where instruction is conducted in Spanish in the morning and in English in the afternoon allows the teacher to introduce a game in Spanish in the morning and a similar game in English in the afternoon. When children hear that "I spy something big, green, and round" is equivalent to "*Veo, veo, algo grande, verde, y redondo,*" they learn more abstract aspects of language and the idea that not everything translates directly. Cross-language spaces will be important in all settings and are likely to enhance the language skills that children bring from home. With this in mind, what are implications for effective practices for DLLs? Table 2.2 illustrates the impact of exposure to dual language instruction on diverse aspects of child development.

Adapting Strategies for Children with Disabilities

Children with specific disabilities such as intellectual disabilities, which often emerge during infancy and toddlerhood, may often display characteristics such as delay in developing language skills (Brillante 2017). In this case, purposeful focus on meaning is a useful strategy because it is specific, and it centers on actions

Ideas for Enhancing the Quality of Language Experiences

> In addition to providing specific names for objects, it is a good idea to directly point to those objects when pronouncing the word. This will increase the likelihood that associations between object and name will be made.

> If additional opportunities to name the same object arise, try adding descriptive words (adjectives) to enrich the experience (e.g., "The hollow twig floats").

Extension Activities for Children with Disabilities

> In addition to focusing on future steps, it is useful to reflect on previous actions (e.g., "Why do you think the large rock sank?").

> Use the environment to encourage associations. For example, after throwing the rock in the water, have children decide which other objects present in the environment will also sink when thrown into the water.

Table 2.2. Language Development: Implications of Dual Language Instructional Strategies

Key Aspects of Language Development	Implications
Ability to distinguish phonemic aspects of two languages	Dual language learning (exposure to two languages at a time) does not compromise preschoolers' ability to learn how words are constructed using different phoneme sequences in two languages or more.
Ability to acquire two languages at preschool age	Systematic exposure to English is critical and must be balanced. DLLs who are exposed to English often show a preference for this language and run the risk of losing command of their home language. Balanced input in both languages is critical.
Ability to develop cognitive proficiency in both languages	Preschool-age DLLs are likely to show significant cognitive growth in both languages when teachers immerse them in meaningful, challenging experiences in which quality language input is provided.

(NASEM 2017).

as they occur. Going back to our earlier example, when observing young children experimenting with objects that float or sink, Ms. Young may provide specific feedback directly connected to the task performed ("Mary, you picked up a large rock. Now you are ready to throw it in the water. What do you predict will happen?"). This statement highlights actions as they occur, but they also anticipate the child's next steps, helping her focus while learning language. For children with disabilities, a focus on meaning while anticipating subsequent actions or events provides a bridge that allows them to remain engaged.

Summary

With your knowledge of what it means to be a dual language learner, you are now better prepared to distinguish between a sequential and a simultaneous bilingual learner. The complex linguistic repertoires of DLLs can be developed in a variety of contexts, including at home and in the educational setting. In essence, all children benefit from responsive teaching that promotes an emphasis on meaning and cognitive engagement.

If we begin to see language as a skill that children will gradually develop and construct with guidance from peers and adults, we, as educators, will be more likely to design educational experiences that actively engage children and challenge them academically regardless of language background. Focusing on meaning and creating cross-language spaces will nurture children's natural inclination to prioritize communication. Therefore, rather than centering on language, we can begin to ask, "In what ways can we implement strategies that support language acquisition while maintaining the cognitive challenges?"

Key Points to Remember!

> Despite concerns regarding children's ability to develop two languages at a young age, we know that all children can be educated bilingually without negative effects (NASEM 2017).

> Children develop vocabulary or their semantic knowledge in formal and informal contexts.

Frequently Asked Questions

What if I speak a different variety of the English or home language spoken by my students? What if I do not speak the language(s) spoken by my students?

Because of the rich linguistic diversity found in most educational settings, all educators are likely to encounter a mismatch between the language they speak and the languages spoken by children in their classrooms. Although some languages may be significantly different (e.g., Russian and Spanish), we are reminded that many varieties of the English language can also be found in the languages DLLs speak. A pre-kindergarten classroom in Dallas, Texas, for example, may include Spanish speakers from Mexico, Puerto Rico, Colombia, and Spain or English speakers from all geographical areas of the country. Key to these common scenarios is the concept of *linguistically accommodated instruction,* sheltered instruction, or instruction that is comprehensible (see Chapter 7). In other words, as an educator, you adopt teaching strategies that combine spoken words, visual representations, changes in speech rate, concrete examples, and activities to provide a rich context as you teach, respond, and facilitate learning.

How long does it take to acquire proficiency in another language?

There are two types of language proficiency. Jim Cummins (2000) made a distinction between the language that allows us to function in social settings, known as *social or conversational language,* and the language that we use in decontextualized academic situations, known as *academic language.* Proficiency in conversational language can be achieved in a relatively short time, generally two years. Academic proficiency in a second language, on the other hand, may take from five to seven years. Children's ability to engage in social conversations in English is often mistaken with their ability to function academically in English, which leads to misconceptions regarding their academic achievement.

References

Bialystok, E. 2015. "Bilingualism and the Development of Executive Function: The Role of Attention." *Child Development Perspectives* 9 (2): 117–21.

Brillante, P. 2017. *The Essentials*: Supporting *Young Children with Disabilities in the Classroom*. Washington, DC: NAEYC.

Collier, V., & W. Thomas. 2009. *Educating English Language Learners for a Transformed World*. Albuquerque, NM: Fuente Press.

Cummins, J. 2000. *Language, Power, and Pedagogy: Bilingual Children in the Crossfire*. Clevedon, UK: Multilingual Matters.

Dombro, A.L., J. Jablon, & C. Stetson. 2020. *Powerful Interactions: How to Connect with Children to Extend Their Learning*. 2nd ed. Washington, DC: NAEYC.

Escamilla, K., S. Hopewell, S. Butvilofsky, W. Sparrow, L. Soltero-González, O. Ruiz-Figueroa, & M. Escamilla. 2014. *Biliteracy from the Start*. Philadelphia: Caslon.

García, O., & L. Wei. 2014. *Translanguaging: Language, Bilingualism and Education*. New York: Palgrave Macmillan.

MacSwan, J. 2017. "A Multilingual Perspective on Translanguaging." *American Educational Research Journal* 54 (1): 167–201.

NASEM (National Academies of Sciences, Engineering, and Medicine). 2017. *Promoting the Educational Success of Children and Youth Learning English: Promising Futures*. Washington, DC: National Academies Press. doi:10.17226/24677.

Otto, B. 2018. *Language Development in Early Childhood*. Upper Saddle River, NJ: Pearson.

Ramírez-Esparza, N., A. García-Sierra, & P.K. Kuhl. 2016. "The Impact of Early Social Interactions on Later Language Development in Spanish–English Bilingual Infants." *Child Development* 88 (4): 1216–34.

naeyc Accreditation
Early Learning Programs

This chapter supports the following NAEYC Early Learning Program Accreditation Standards and Topic Areas:

Standard 2: Curriculum
2.D Language Development

Standard 3: Teaching
3.A Designing Enriched Language Environments
3.F Making Learning Meaningful for All Learners

3 What Should I Consider When Implementing a Dual Language Program?

Objectives

> Identify goals of dual language programs.

> Describe language allocation in dual language classrooms.

> Discuss differences between language of instruction, language of learning, and language of communication.

> Analyze strategies for language input in dual language early childhood settings.

Ms. Martínez has just started a new position as a dual language teacher at an early childhood center. On the first day of school, she noticed that children in her classroom were using their home language (Spanish) during English instruction. At the end of the day, she asked her colleague, Ms. Olvera, if it was appropriate to switch the language of instruction to match the language used by her preschoolers during her English read-alouds. Ms. Olvera explained that it was in the children's best interest if she remained in the language of instruction but encouraged her to make sure the selected reading included visuals that connected to the children's prior experiences.

Early childhood educators such as Ms. Martínez encounter multiple decision-making moments related to use of language on a daily basis. Unlike the preceding scenario, the implementation of early childhood dual language programs across the country is more the exception than the rule. This leaves educators with many questions regarding the best way to promote and support the goal of biliteracy, bilingualism, and bicultural competence for all children (NASEM 2017).

Since the passage of the Bilingual Education Act of 1968, educators have implemented a variety of bilingual programs (see www.cal.org to learn more). Dual language programs fall under the umbrella of additive bilingual education programs in which teachers provide grade-level content and literacy instruction to all children in two languages. These are designated as **one-way** or

one-way dual language program
Program that includes speakers of one language group (e.g., Spanish, Vietnamese, Chinese) who are learning content in two languages.

two-way dual language program
Program that includes speakers of two language groups (e.g., Spanish-dominant children and English-dominant children participate in balanced numbers) who are learning content in two languages.

two-way dual language programs. Literacy is acquired in both languages either simultaneously or with an initial emphasis on home language literacy. This chapter focuses on program goals, considerations for language allocation, types of language input, and characteristics of language of instruction, language of learning, and language of communication when implementing a dual language program.

What Are the Goals of Dual Language Programs?

Discussing the goals of dual language programs is important because it reminds us that in the United States, bilingual education emerged as an outcome of a historical quest for social justice—that is, "the foundations of the bilingual education field, tell a story of struggle for access to equitable educational resources" (Fitts & Weisman 2010, 374), privileges, and opportunities to advance academically. In linguistically and culturally diverse early childhood settings, a social justice orientation translates into a commitment to value, maintain, and develop the home language while supporting acquisition of the English language. Scholars agree that three foundational goals of dual language education include the following (Gómez 2000; Howard et al. 2018):

> **Grade-level/developmentally appropriate academic achievement.** In dual language classrooms, educators focus on developmentally appropriate strategies, grade-level objectives, challenging instruction, research-based strategies, and comprehensible input in both languages.

> **Bilingualism and biliteracy.** Early childhood educators understand that language acquisition and development is a process. Strategic planning is in place to provide quality exposure to both languages, and predictable opportunities are designed to engage children in all modes of language activity, including listening, speaking, reading, and writing.

> **Sociocultural competence and positive cross-cultural perspectives.** Knowledge of customs, cultures, and household practices is closely connected to the school curriculum. Program directors, educators, and families work together to prepare children as they know and appreciate their own culture and that of their classmates.

Language Allocation in Early Childhood Dual Language Settings for 3- to 5-Year-Olds

An ideal language model for dual language learners ages 3 to 5 considers aspects related to the specific context in which the program will be implemented. In other words, educators are encouraged to investigate the cultural, linguistic, and socioeconomic factors that shape the schools where they teach (e.g., languages spoken in the community, celebrations, occupations, and patterns of interactions). This entails establishing connections with families in the community to ensure that the school climate and curriculum allow young children to continue developing a strong bilingual and bicultural identity. Once you have made the decision to adopt an instructional model that seeks to achieve academic excellence, bilingualism and biliteracy, and cultural competence, your next decision will be about language allocation. How will educators allocate the home language and the English language throughout the instructional day? Will you use a 90:10 ratio (90 percent of instruction in the home language and 10 percent of instruction in English) or a 50:50 ratio (balanced use of English and Spanish for instructional purposes)?

Most dual language models provide guidance for language allocation decisions that make sense in K–12 settings but may fail to consider the developmental needs of preschool-age children. In K–12 settings, dual language learners are clearly ready to engage in more sophisticated aspects of language production. Young children (ages 3–5), on the other hand, rely heavily on adults as language models. A key aspect at this stage of development is children's dependence on adults' use of encouragement and responsiveness as children gradually take risks with language.

> ### Language Practices in Local Dual Language Schools
>
> › Identify an early childhood dual language program in your local context. Review their website and locate information related to language allocation. This will allow you to familiarize yourself with ways in which programs distribute use of languages for instruction. What do you notice?

Language Use in Preschool Settings: Focus on Conversational Language

Language planning should actively involve children in conversations. Simply stated, children should engage as active participants in listening, taking conversational turns, and using different modes of communication (e.g., gestures, drawings). As you consider the language use within your context, how will adults use that language? When, how, and for what purpose will they use each language? These questions can help guide our decisions regarding language allocation for DLLs. Other important questions to consider include:

> What language will families speak at home?

> How will language be allocated at home?

> How will language experiences at home align with language experiences in the educational or formal setting?

> How will language experiences at home and educational settings connect with culture and DLL identity formation?

What Is the Difference Between Language of Instruction, Language of Learning, and Language of Informal Communication in Dual Language Settings?

translanguaging
To alternate language codes for meaningful purposes to communicate without concern about adhering to a prescribed language. May involve alternation of languages, as well as use of other resources (gestures, visual resources, languages, etc.) to convey meaning: "I ♥ you. You are my favorite *tío* (uncle)."

codeswitching
The practice of alternating languages within a conversation. Example: "I am feeling a little *confundido* (confused)."

The language that adults use at home is as critical to the bilingual development of DLLs as is the language used in the classroom. At the heart of a dual language program design is the overall goal of bilingualism and biliteracy aligned with high academic outcomes. How to achieve this goal is a complex decision that leads to varied model designs, hopefully driven by particular conditions within the context. Several features are proposed as guidelines to plan and monitor dual language programs. These features directly guide assessment and accountability, curriculum and instructional practices, staff quality and professional development, program structure, family and community involvement, and support and resources. This section zeroes in on the types of language found in dual language settings, including language of instruction, language of learning, and language of informal communication.

Language of Instruction

The language used by the teacher for the purpose of presenting content and accomplishing language-related goals is known as *language of instruction*. For example, when Mrs. Díaz begins her English math lesson, she uses English as her language of instruction. Throughout her mathematics block of time, she remains in English. This type of language input is critical for development of all types of language knowledge (phonological, semantic, syntactic, morphemic, and pragmatic). A consistent monolingual delivery allows for predictable exposure to children's first and second language. It also places the teacher as the language model systematically using vocabulary, grammatical structures in contextually language rich experiences (Howard et al. 2018).

Language of Learning

The language(s) that children use to construct meaning and communicate new understandings is known as the *language of learning* (Arreguín-Anderson & Alanís 2019). As DLLs engage in meaningful experiences, they begin to build a vast language repertoire. As discussed in Chapter 2, some of those experiences may have taken place in English, while others in Spanish.

As they learn, DLLs engage in **translanguaging** practices; in other words, they dynamically use features of all languages they know to construct meaning (García & Wei 2014). In practice, the expressive language or language of learning DLLs use may often show complex structures from two languages, also known as **codeswitching.** Let's refer to the earlier example. Although Mrs. Díaz is using English as her language of instruction, children are free to use either their first or second language or both (codeswitching) for their negotiation of meaning. Gradually, the language of DLLs evolves to match the teacher's modeled input.

Language of Informal Communication

Language of informal communication refers to the social, informal language used outside of academic contexts. The definition Cummins (2000) used for **basic interpersonal communication skills** is useful in distinguishing between language that DLLs know and use for informal conversations and the academic language known as **cognitive academic language proficiency**. When you observe children playing or communicating in informal settings, you will notice that the language used at the interpersonal level, with friends and family, tends to adjust to the dynamics present in those social circles. In other words, children understand that language is fluid. It is important for educators to understand the difference between social and academic language because DLLs may be less verbal when required to use academic language that has just been introduced and in the context of cognitively difficult tasks. To support dual language development, educators are encouraged to make instruction comprehensible (see Chapter 7).

basic interpersonal communication skills
Skills that allow us to efficiently interact in everyday social interactions. Example: "How was your weekend?"

cognitive academic language proficiency
Proficiency in the language used in the classroom for the purpose of expressing learning in the content areas (e.g., mathematics, social studies, science). Example: "Compare and contrast liquids and solids."

Strategies for Language Input in Dual Language Early Childhood Settings

Although responsiveness and adult stimulation can be broadly defined as being attentive and encouraging, DLLs benefit from interactions with adults who systematically use rich descriptive language. Quality language input does not happen by accident. Initially, careful planning should go into decisions related to:

> The language that will be used and when to use it (language allocation)

> The design of class schedules to ensure a minimum of 50 percent exposure to children's home languages

While quantity of exposure to both languages is important, language planning in early childhood settings must go beyond basic language allocation or beyond a general program type indicating a 50:50 or 90:10 distribution. The language used by the teacher—the language of instruction—is powerful, as it directly enhances children's receptive vocabulary. In early childhood dual language settings, educators must pay close attention to language of instruction or language input that is representational, interactional, and imaginative.

Representational Language

Because the instructional day is intentionally planned, early childhood dual language educators purposefully use language to name, describe, and explain. As discussed in Chapter 2, young learners acquire vocabulary in different contexts, in different languages, and with different individuals. In your role as educator, what vocabulary and expressions will DLLs learn when they spend time with you? More specifically, how will you describe events, objects, and actions produced or provided in the presence of the child?

Representational language is powerful because it equips us with nouns and adjectives for objects and events that are relevant in the immediate context. One pattern of interaction that focuses on description of objects and actions is *verbal mapping* which is an oral identification of the concepts being experienced as children use their senses and share discoveries (Otto 2018; Salinas González, Arreguín-Anderson, & Alanís 2018). Support for verbal mapping comes from research highlighting the importance of actively engaging children's interests, exposing them to experiences, and being attentive to their actions and immediately labeling those actions and objects (Salinas González et al. 2018).

Interactional Language

Interactional language is the glue that allows us to begin carrying out formal and informal social and academic tasks. It can also be defined as the language that we use to engage with others. Because learning is a social endeavor, continuous modeling of interactional language is key to children's development of academic and socioemotional skills. When adults purposefully model interactional language, it allows children to learn and appropriate language that is needed to engage in dialogue, discussions, and small group interactions (Alanís & Arreguín-Anderson 2019). Interactional language is essential and should begin as early as possible, even with infant DLLs who are not ready to verbally respond but who will respond through vocalizations or nonverbal responses.

In dual language settings, children and adults interact with each other as they begin their daily routines, transition from one lesson or activity to another, and complete group work or partner-based work. In Table 3.1, we provide examples of the language children might use with each other in a classroom that provides 50 percent of instructional time in English and 50 percent of instructional time in the home language. These purposeful interactions result in cross-cultural connections as children are exposed to the intricacies of language and culture in an authentic context.

Table 3.1. Examples of Interactional Language

Interactional Language	Day of the Week	Language
Greeting: *¡Buenos días! ¿Cómo amaneciste?*	Monday, Wednesday, and Friday	Spanish
Good morning! How are you this morning?	Tuesday and Thursday	English
Small Group Skills: *¿En qué te puedo ayudar?*	Monday, Wednesday, and Friday	Spanish
How can I help you?	Monday through Friday	English

Imaginative Language

Language that is used to create, explore, and entertain aligns with young children's inclination to imagine and play. Interactions that involve DLLs in storytelling and pretend play scenarios support semantic development and acquisition of expressive skills. Imaginative language permeates traditional storytelling and oral traditions embedded in many cultural groups that include vivid narratives in their informal communications. Adults who tell stories and use engaging phrases (e.g., "Let's pretend . . .," "Once upon a time . . .," "The other day I touched a star and it was . . .") enrich young children's expressive language skills. Gradually, children transition from an initial engagement in receptive language to a more sophisticated role as users and producers of language.

Summary

Dual language models differ in terms of exposure to the home language and English. The goals of a dual language program include biliteracy, bilingualism, and cultural competence. These goals are achieved when language allocation or distribution of languages (English and the home language) is strategically planned and consistently adhered to. In general, early childhood educators play a key role as language models. When adults use representational, interactional, and imaginative language, it equips young learners with a vast linguistic repertoire in both languages. Early childhood educators must also ensure that the language of instruction and the language of learning are clearly outlined in favor of children's language development.

Key Points to Remember!

> Language planning should actively involve children in conversations. Simply stated, children should engage as active participants by listening, taking conversational turns, and using different modes of communication (e.g., gestures, drawings).

> The language used by the teacher for the purpose of presenting content and accomplishing language-related goals is known as the *language of instruction*.

> The language(s) that children use to construct meaning and communicate new understandings is known as the *language of learning* (Arreguín-Anderson & Alanís 2019).

> *Language of communication* refers to the social, informal language used outside of academic contexts.

Frequently Asked Questions

What types of professional development do my teachers need?

Professional development for teachers in a dual language program should focus on effective strategies to make instruction comprehensible while maintaining the cognitive demand of the task, interactive/cooperative learning, and linguistically accommodated strategies. Another critical topic is the use of culturally relevant teaching approaches. This involves incorporating aspects of children's lives into daily instruction with the goal of infusing relevancy and validating children's cultural identities.

Do all my teachers need to be bilingual?

Educational early childhood settings that seek to implement a dual language program generally have bilingual staff (bilingual speakers of main language groups). A successful dual language program can also be operated in settings where one teacher is fluent in English or is a monolingual English speaker and other teachers are fluent speakers of the partner language of instruction (National Center on Cultural and Linguistic Responsiveness 2015). Team planning is critical to the success of dual language programs in order to coordinate learning objectives and ensure rigor.

References

Alanís, I., & M.G. Arreguín-Anderson. 2019. "Paired Learning: Strategies for Enhancing Social Competence in Dual Language Classrooms." *Young Children* 74 (2): 6–12.

Arreguín-Anderson, M.G., & I. Alanís. 2019. *Translingual Partners in Early Childhood Elementary-Education: Pedagogies on Linguistic and Cognitive Engagement.* New York: Peter Lang Publishing.

Cummins, J. 2000. *Language, Power, and Pedagogy: Bilingual Children in the Crossfire.* Clevedon, UK: Multilingual Matters.

Fitts, S., & E.M. Weisman. 2010. "Exploring Questions of Social Justice in Bilingual/Bicultural Teacher Education: Towards a Parity of Participation." *Urban Review* 42 (5): 373–93. doi:10.1007/s11256-009-0139-9.

García, O., & L. Wei. 2014. *Translanguaging: Language, Bilingualism, and Education.* New York: Palgrave Macmillan.

Gómez, L. 2000. "Two-Way Bilingual Education: Promoting Educational and Social Change." *Journal of the Texas Association for Bilingual Education* 5 (1): 43–54.

Howard, E.R., K.J. Lindholm-Leary, D. Rogers, N. Olague, J. Medina, B. Kennedy, J. Sugarman, & D. Christian. 2018. *Guiding Principles for Dual Language Education.* 3rd ed. Washington, DC: Center for Applied Linguistics; Albuquerque, NM: Dual Language Education of New Mexico; Miami, FL: Santillana USA.

NASEM (National Academies of Sciences, Engineering, and Medicine). 2017. *Promoting the Educational Success of Children and Youth Learning English: Promising Futures.* Washington, DC: National Academies Press. doi:10.17226/24677.

National Center on Cultural and Linguistic Responsiveness. 2015. *Classroom Language Models: A Leaders' Implementation Manual.* Report prepared for the US Department of Health and Human Services, Administration for Children and Families, Office of Head Start. Washington, DC: US Department of Health and Human Services, Administration for Children and Families, Office of Head Start. https://eclkc.ohs.acf.hhs.gov/sites/default/files/pdf/pps-language-models.pdf.

Otto, B. 2018. *Language Development in Early Childhood.* Upper Saddle River, NJ: Pearson.

Salinas González, I., M.G. Arreguín-Anderson, & I. Alanís. 2018. "Supporting Language: Culturally Rich Dramatic Play." *Teaching Young Children* 11 (2): 4–6.

Accreditation
Early Learning Programs

This chapter supports the following NAEYC Early Learning Program Accreditation Standards and topic areas:

Standard 2: Curriculum
2.D Language Development
2.E Early Literacy

Standard 3: Teaching
3.F Making Learning Meaningful for All Children

Supporting Learning
and Development

4 Creating Culturally and Linguistically Diverse Environments

Objectives

> Illustrate components of a culturally and linguistically responsive environment.

> Discuss families as resources for this environment.

> Identify materials and spaces that support dual language learners in the classroom.

> Describe the use of environmental resources: labels, signs, word walls, child-created alphabets.

> Identify essential supports for dual language learners: schedules, routines, and transitions.

> Describe how to develop an inclusive learning environment for dual language learners.

As you walk toward the Sunshine Learning Center preschool classroom, you see pictures of diverse families displayed in the hallway with a *Welcome* heading in English, Spanish, and Vietnamese. Inside the classroom, there is a large group meeting area with a colorful rug and smaller areas with child-size furniture. The large group meeting area has pictures on the wall representing the children in the classroom with their names placed at the children's eye level. The smaller sections of the classroom are clearly visible and have a variety of learning centers labeled as *Dramatic Play, Library, Literacy, Construction, Creative Art, Music and Movement, Discovery,* and *Quiet Time Area.* These learning centers are labeled and color-coded in three languages representing the children in the classroom. As you explore, you see a variety of multicultural books in the children's home languages, materials from children's homes, and open-ended and close-ended resources. Just as you start to wonder where the children and their teachers are, you see a schedule on the main wall with pictures of the children depicting their daily activities. You figure it out—they are outside at this time! You peek through the window and there they are giggling with the teacher as they are playing with *rebozos* (pashminas or shawls) as their teacher chants, "*¿El rebozo, el rebozo, dónde está, dónde está?*" (The shawl, the shawl, where is it, where is it?) to the tune of "Where Is Thumbkin?"

Early childhood environments, such as the one described at the Sunshine Learning Center, have a crucial impact on how comfortable and secure young children feel, especially for DLLs who may be experiencing their first environment outside their home and in a language they do not understand. The children's environment includes the content educators arrange in the classroom, the atmosphere they create, and the feeling they communicate within that environment (Gordon & Browne 2017). A carefully planned environment, as in the opening vignette, supports children's learning and literacy development while also valuing their languages and culture. For example, DLLs and their families could see themselves reflected in the materials displayed in the learning centers and in the photos inside the classroom and in the hallway. It clearly conveyed a welcoming feeling to preschoolers and their families by acknowledging their language, culture, and abilities.

In this chapter, we discuss how environments for DLLs are culturally and linguistically responsive and convey to children that adults value and care for them. We explore how families can contribute to a culturally relevant classroom environment. We follow with a description of how resources, materials, and spaces included in the classroom contribute to the socioemotional, language, and literacy development of DLLs and how teachers can guide and structure their classroom. Finally, we offer ideas for creating an inclusive classroom environment for DLLs with various abilities. You will see how these links come together to create an environment where DLLs can succeed.

Environments for DLLs Are Culturally and Linguistically Responsive

Children's development and learning is influenced by their social, linguistic, and cultural contexts (Espinosa 2015). These contexts include children's interactions with their family, educators, and their daily community experiences. Responsive educators are knowledgeable of their children's home languages and cultures and use this knowledge

to plan learning environments that support bilingual and bicultural development (Castro, Espinosa, & Páez 2011; Genesee, Paradis, & Crago 2004). When educators commit to providing a responsive environment, they take time to know each child's language, family, and culture. By doing this, DLLs feel valued and safe while being intellectually stimulated.

Families' Cultural Capital Informs a Language-Rich Environment

As discussed in earlier chapters, children's families, culture, and home context influence childrearing, learning and language development, and the interactions they have with adults in their lives. Understanding and respecting the familial culture of DLLs is crucial in building a foundation for providing an environment that nurtures children's overall well-being. Responsive educators acknowledge children's **cultural capital** and collaborate with families to create a space that focuses on their unique skills, strengths, and experiences (Yosso 2005). The home and community experiences that children bring to the classroom are considered resources that contribute to their **funds of knowledge** (Gonzalez, Moll, & Amanti 2005; Moll et al. 1992). Educators can acquire information about children's funds of knowledge through home visits, observing children in their care, or informal interviews (García 2003; Moll et al. 1992). In the following section, we discuss how family photographs and resources from home are two ways to connect with children's cultural wealth.

cultural capital

Unique skills, strengths, and experiences that DLLs possess.

funds of knowledge

Essential cultural practices and bodies of knowledge that are part of the daily practices and routines of families, including family and community experiences, traditions, and resources (NAEYC 2019).

Family and Community Photographs

The resources from home and the community become endless opportunities to develop language and literacy for DLLs. For example, in Mr. Lopez's kindergarten classroom, we found teacher-made puzzles of family photographs. During their study on vegetables, one of the children shared a photo of her dad working in a pumpkin field. (She was one of several DLLs in Mr. Lopez's classroom who had a family that migrated for work.) Mr. Lopez enlarged the picture, laminated it, and made it into a puzzle during their study on vegetables. Children in his classroom enjoyed putting the puzzle together and asking questions about migrant farmworkers. The culturally relevant puzzle portrayed the child's culture in a positive and realistic way while providing many opportunities for language development. Most importantly, it gave the children of migrant farmworkers a sense of pride while learning.

Using Family Photos and Artifacts

> Families may contribute photographs or objects that can decorate the classroom bulletin boards, make games, or be placed at the writing center. For example, when talking about special family events, children may bring objects or pictures depicting the diverse events they participate in regularly.

Family-Generated Alphabet

Instead of displaying commercially developed alphabets populated with images that have little connection to the children in your classroom, we recommend developing a family-generated alphabet and then a child-created alphabet (Arreguín-Anderson, Alanís, & Salinas-González 2016) in two phases, as shown in Figure 4.1. The family-generated alphabet, provides children the opportunity to work together with their families as they develop an alphabet for the classroom based on resources provided from home. Educators assign different letters to each child as they look for items or pictures from home that start with the assigned letter. For example, Aditi glued a label for *Karachi* cookies

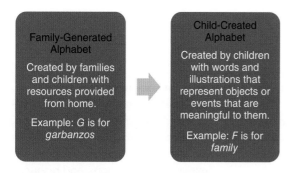

Figure 4.1. A family-generated alphabet provides children the opportunity to work together with their families as they develop an alphabet for the classroom based on resources provided from home. Child-created alphabets empower DLLs to think of familiar words and images that emerge from their family, community, or classroom experiences.

Creating Children's Albums

> Place children's photographs in an album where children may choose a photograph to draw or write about during learning center time.

> Have children share their drawing or writing with their peers.

Creating Thematic Classroom Alphabets

> Create a classroom alphabet after a school field trip to describe what children saw, touched, heard, or smelled. For example, after a visit to a local nature center, children may decide to add *A* for *ants, B* for *butterflies, C* for *cactus,* and so on.

on the letter *K*. This is a common word that she has heard at home, as her grandmother brings these cookies every time she visits. Ana glued a label for *Abuelita* chocolate on the letter *A*. This alphabet activity leads to alphabet knowledge, phonological awareness, and print awareness through meaningful connections to their familiar cultural capital. DLLs develop a sense of competence and enjoyment when sharing their home resources.

Child-Created Alphabets

Alphabetic awareness, together with phonemic awareness, vocabulary, and concepts of print, are identified as predictors of literacy development for DLLs (National Early Literacy Panel 2008; Tabors 2008). Many children, however, will start preschool or kindergarten reading their environment without being able to identify individual letters of the alphabet. Child-created alphabets empower DLLs to think of familiar words and images that emerge from their family, community, or classroom experiences. For example, after a class discussion on what makes our families unique, each child may be given a paper with a letter of the alphabet and a blank space for them to write words or create illustrations that describe what makes their family unique, such as *B* for *bilingual, C* for *cook, L* for *loving,* and so on. Children's direct participation will contribute to their understanding of individual phonemes in words that they have experienced and that have meaning to them and their families.

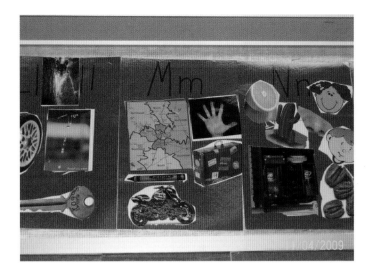

Materials and Spaces That Support DLLs in the Classroom

It is important for educators to select books, posters, puzzles, toys, and games that represent the cultural diversity of the classroom (Espinosa 2015). Not all materials are culturally neutral. Consider the language, race, ethnicity, family structure, disabilities, and occupations of the families in your early childhood program. By incorporating materials that feature the diverse aspects of the children and families you serve, you send the message that diversity is valued while at the same time setting a foundation for literacy learning opportunities that children can connect to.

When selecting materials, resources, and displays, consider the following:

> Integrate toys, games, bulletin boards, songs, poems, rhymes, and chants that represent children in your context.

> Create a multilingual library center that represents children's culture, experiences, and languages in books and storytelling puppets.

> Include photographs, illustrations, posters, and graphics that accurately reflect the children in your classroom.

> Include children's languages on classroom labels, word walls, alphabets, signs, and bulletin boards. Color-code them for easy visual discrimination.

(Adapted from National Center on Cultural and Linguistic Responsiveness 2020)

Using Labels from Children's Homes

> Label a small plastic bag with a letter from the alphabet and send it home to each family.

> Ask them to place labels or wrappers of some of the foods found at home that start with the letter on the bag.

> The families will return a variety of labels of many foods, including vegetables, beans, cereal, rice, orzo, and juices, to name a few.

> Use the labels to create a family-generated alphabet, place the labels on the word wall, make a class book about the foods in children's homes, or create a collage on a bulletin board titled "A to Z Labels from Home."

Include Learning Centers

Developmentally appropriate early childhood educators divide the classroom environment into defined areas where children can work in small groups with multisensory activities that provide opportunities for language and content development. These small areas are typically called **learning centers,** *interest centers, learning stations,* or *workstations.* Ensure that learning centers intentionally focus on the developing language skills of DLLs. Some examples include the dramatic play center, the writing center, the literacy center, the listening center, the computer center, the construction center, the library center, the math center, the discovery center (science), and the creative arts center (see Chapter 9 for center descriptions).

learning centers
Designated areas within the classroom that address various subjects and include a variety of hands-on learning opportunities.

Learning Centers Benefit DLLs

Educators carefully plan meaningful activities placed in each learning center to fully engage all DLLs in play-based learning. This affords DLLs with many opportunities to engage in learning new concepts and practicing their language, including the following benefits:

> Provide opportunities for children to scaffold each other's language and learning as they work in pairs or small groups (Alanís 2013).

> Support their full language abilities (García & Wei 2014).

> Create an opportunity for teachers to provide individualized support when needed.

> Reinforce and refine concepts being learned.

> Encourage increased engagement while enhancing language opportunities.

> Provide hands-on and minds-on learning through diverse materials, games, and resources.

> Address children's diverse learning styles, individual needs, and interests (Magruder et al. 2013).

DLLs benefit from having child-initiated experiences in learning centers that last an extended period of time—Epstein (2014) recommends 45 to 90 minutes of learning centers daily—to fully engage in concept development. To maximize learning for DLLs, there are also learning center guidelines to consider.

Guidelines to Consider When Arranging a Learning Center Environment for DLLs

> Include task cards with illustrations that guide children on how to use the learning center materials.

> Establish a limit on the number of children who work in each center at a time to maintain focus and productive interactions among children.

> Make sure that all learning centers provide materials in English and children's home languages. Color-code them for easy identification.

> Group learning centers according to content to create opportunities for more enriched play. For example, place STEM (science [discovery], technology, engineering [construction], and mathematics) centers close to each other and literacy centers (library, writing, literacy) next to each other.

> Integrate literacy materials in all learning centers (e.g., books, variety of writing tools, paper).

> Provide culturally relevant learning games and activities in all learning centers.

> Arrange learning centers for easy visibility of all children to guide them as needed.

> Ensure clear pathways and accessibility to learning centers for children with disabilities.

Resources That Support DLLs Within the Classroom

As we will discuss in Chapter 5, a literate classroom environment is infused with language and print. Classrooms for DLLs include both environmental print and functional print that reflect children's home languages and English to create a supportive linguistic environment. **Environmental print** is a child's first recognizable print as their literacy skills begin to develop. This type of print is found in children's familiar surroundings and in their community.

Writing with Colored Salt

> Dye salt with food coloring in a gallon-size plastic bag and place it in a shoebox for children to practice writing in the writing center.

> We recommend creating two boxes with different-colored salt for children to practice writing in English and in their home language.

environmental print
Familiar print that surrounds us on a daily basis found on labels, signs, packaging, and road signs.

functional print
Print communication information that is purposeful and instructional.

It may be found at restaurants, in stores, in the home, or outside on the road. This includes logos, food labels, and road signs. On the other hand, **functional print** provides visual supports that help DLLs navigate the classroom environment. Functional print visually connects written language with objects, directions, and routines. It assists DLLs to decipher the environment even if they are not speaking or reading the language (Espinosa 2015). It provides them with opportunities to use language in both the spoken and written form while contributing to children's understanding of the words they hear and the connections between those words and the labels found around the classroom (Salinas-González, Arreguín-Anderson, & Alanís 2015).

Functional Print in a Dual Language Classroom

Educators of DLLs intentionally promote language and literacy opportunities through the use of the environment. Functional print sends the message that print is purposeful and provides valuable information to DLLs trying to make sense of their classroom environment. Effective teachers thoughtfully plan a print-rich environment where DLLs can playfully explore literacy-enhancing materials (Roskos & Neuman 2001), resources, and visuals in two languages. In the following sections, we describe examples of how educators create language and literacy opportunities for DLLs.

Interactive Labels

Labels serve as visual supports of print and vocabulary knowledge in children's home language and in English. Labels contribute to the development of autonomy and help children make sense of their classroom surroundings, including learning centers, school supplies, educational resources, cubbies, calendar, furniture, lunch menu, and other crucial classroom materials. For example, labeling the list of classroom helpers identifies children's duties for the day. As shown in figure, these visual references assist children in identifying who will help the teacher, where to find materials, where to put them away, and how to keep their environment organized. This will nurture a sense of competency in DLLs as they start reading and navigating their environment in two languages or more.

Guidelines to Consider When Labeling

> Color-code the print on the labels to help DLLs distinguish between English and their home language.

> Place labels at children's eye level to make them accessible and interactive.

> Involve children in creating and placing the labels to help them make literacy connections.

> Add important labels to the calendar, such as special celebrations or days. This helps children anticipate future events.

> Conduct daily "environment literacy walks" in English and in children's home language, if possible.

> Pair children as they walk around the classroom and read labels or words from the word wall.

> Strategically place labels in the classroom environment to encourage children to read, touch, remove, and play with them (Salinas-González, Arreguín-Anderson, & Alanís 2015).

Functional Signs

Signs in the classroom communicate information and provide directions to support children's independence. Use a combination of words and an illustration that represents the word(s). Additionally, read the signs with children and have them repeat the word with you as you place the sign in spaces that are visible and accessible. For example, in a Spanish–English classroom, you may create signs for "Line starts here/*La fila empieza aquí*," "Exit/*Salida*," "Work in progress/*Trabajo en proceso*," "Clean up/*Limpiar*," "Center Closed/*Centro cerrado*," "Girls' restroom/*Baño de niñas*," "Quiet voice/*Voz baja*," "Wash your hands/*Lávate las manos*," "Partner work/*Trabajo en pareja*," or "Walk/*Caminar*."

Involving Children in Classroom Letter Searches

> Give children pointers or fly swatters and involve them in finding words in their classroom that have certain letter sounds.

> Ask children to find all the words that begin with the same letter or end with the same letter as their name.

Interactive Word Walls

A word wall is a literacy tool that assists DLLs with reading and writing (Fountas & Pinnell 2010). It includes the letters of the alphabet and a space to display words across a wall in the main area of the classroom. Word walls should be interactive for children and should be at eye level so that children have visual and physical access to the words as needed. At first, young children may help you add their names to the word wall in alphabetical order. Later, you can involve them in adding words that you have selected and words that

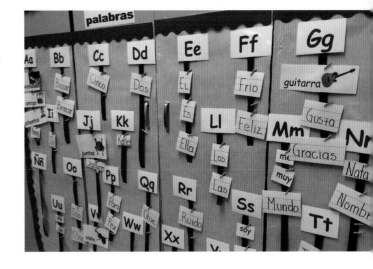

come from children's interests and needs. For example, after observing that many DLLs use a phonetic spelling of *da* for the word *the,* educators may engage children during circle time in adding the commonly misspelled word to the word wall and pointing out its pronunciation and spelling. Separate word walls by language and add pictures to help DLLs identify words in each language even when they cannot decode them (Alanís, Salinas-González, & Arreguín-Anderson 2015).

Encourage DLLs to Interact with Their Environment

Displaying an abundance of print is not sufficient to make print meaningful for DLLs (Love, Burns, & Buell 2007). Children must engage with the print. A responsive classroom environment is predominately a social setting where children are provided with many playful opportunities to interact with their environmental print, the educator, and their peers (Salinas-González, Arreguín-Anderson, & Alanís 2015).

The best way to ensure that the environment becomes a teaching and learning tool is to refer to the words displayed daily and to involve DLLs in concrete explorations of the print. Soon you will notice how they begin to playfully emulate your actions as they point to words and pictures and read them. Print in the classroom environment empowers DLLs to use language in both the spoken and written form through playful and meaningful tasks. Use caution, however, to not overwhelm children with too much print that looks cluttered, haphazard, or lacks intention.

Establish Essential Supports for Dual Language Learners

DLLs benefit from environments that provide essential support with schedules, routines, and transitions. Provide DLLs with verbal and nonverbal supports to help them understand what behaviors are expected from them at different times of the day. When their environment is predictable, it creates a safe, warm, and engaging classroom that is not dependent on understanding and speaking English (National Center on Cultural and Linguistic Responsiveness 2020). Consistency helps DLLs feel safe in their environment and be more willing to participate in classroom interactions with their teachers and peers. Children can anticipate where they can experience positive relationships with others while developing their socioemotional, physical, and intellectual abilities (NASEM 2017). These interactions create positive adult–child relationships, and they affect children's developing sense of self-esteem

(IOM & NRC 2000). Additionally, including a quiet space where DLLs can spend some alone time or take a break from thinking and learning in their second language adds to their socioemotional well-being.

Predictable Schedule

Responsive environments support DLLs by providing a predictable schedule. Maintaining a daily schedule fosters a positive relationship between young children and their teacher as children begin to feel comfortable and see the consistency in their new learning environment (Gonzalez-Mena 2011). Add words and pictures to the schedule to describe the daily activities. Review the schedule with the children at the beginning of the day. Children learn to interpret pictures and start making the connection between the picture and the word. Include the children's languages to reinforce vocabulary in their home language and English. For example, you may place a clothespin with an arrow indicating where you are in the schedule. This helps children identify what is coming next and cues them when an activity is over.

Design a daily schedule that supports development with balanced opportunities for individual and small group learning time as well as child-initiated and teacher-initiated learning time. This provides children with opportunities to interact with their peers and educators as they enhance their home language and practice their emerging English skills. Another consideration is to schedule shorter periods of whole group time for younger DLLs. Group times are most effective when children are engaged in interactive activities like music and movement, puppetry, or drama. Ultimately, the classroom schedule should reflect the developmental, linguistic, and cultural needs of DLLs within your context.

Clear Routines and Transitions

Routines and predictable transitions provide a sense of order to the schedule. DLLs benefit from regular routines that are presented with simple repetitive songs or chants and simple motions or visual cues for transitions (see Chapter 9). Some DLLs may not be familiar with some of the expected transitions, such as sitting in a circle or taking turns, so it is important to model all routine and transition expectations. Once the children learn your expectations for them, you can fade out the routine and allow children to self-monitor (Espinosa 2015).

Figure 4.2. Predictable schedule.

Providing Predictable Schedules

> Create a schedule with visual supports such as pictures or graphics to assist DLLs in knowing what to expect during the day.

> Add a clothespin to identify the time of the day on the schedule.

Creating Consistent Transitions

> Use chants or songs to transition children from finishing a read-aloud to another activity. One example you might use is this popular Spanish chanting rhyme: "Colorín, colorado, esté cuento se a acabado, el que se quede sentado, se queda pegado." In essence, this chant translates to "This colorful story has ended. If you stay seated, you'll stay glued to the floor."

multimodal
Experiences that allow for diverse learners to acquire information using multiple senses and modes of learning.

least restrictive environment (LRE)
Part of the Individuals with Disabilities Education Act (IDEA) that states that children who participate in special education should be educated as much as possible with children without disabilities who do not receive special education.

Individuals with Disabilities Education Act (IDEA)
Federal law governing services for children with disabilities or special needs.

Arrival and Dismissal Routine

A well-prepared environment will ease arrivals and dismissals for DLLs. It may be a challenge to greet each child and her family to "make them feel welcome, exchange information, help with feelings of separation by being understanding, reassuring, and supportive, and watch the rest of the group at the same time" (Gonzalez-Mena 2011, 295). Children's cultures influence their transition when they arrive for the day and again when they leave. Children in new environments respond differently. For some, the presence of a family member may ease the arrival, while others may be comforted by a ritual like a hug from the parent or the educator (Gonzalez-Mena 2011). These moments can provide reassurance as children leave one environment and a set of people for another. Both families and DLLs may feel insecure during the child's arrival at school. Acknowledge these feelings and assure families that their child will be cared for in the early childhood classroom.

Adapting the Environment for DLLs with Disabilities

Educators of DLLs differentiate instruction and modify the classroom environment to ensure that all children experience success. In doing so, educators create multisensory and **multimodal** experiences that are interrelated to ensure mastery of skills and concepts in the **least restrictive environment.** This means that children with disabilities should be educated alongside of children without disabilities, according to Section 612 of **Individuals with Disabilities Education Act (IDEA)** (NASEM 2017). Children with disabilities may only be removed from the regular education classroom when their disabilities prevent them from receiving an adequate education and after they have been provided with individualized supports. Although many of the materials, resources, and strategies presented in this chapter are effective for all DLLs, there are additional guidelines to consider when working with DLLs with disabilities.

Guidelines for Creating an Inclusive Environment

> Adapt materials, resources, and games to allow all children to participate in the learning process.

> Create clear classroom pathways for children to access their word walls, labels, and signs.

> Make materials and resources accessible so DLLs with different abilities see themselves as capable learners.

> Provide peer or adult support.

> Make sure that the classroom environment reflects children with various abilities.

> Display pictures and graphics of children with various abilities in your classroom signs, schedules, and functional print.

> Include books that portray children with disabilities.

> Invite families or community members with disabilities to be guests.

> Observe your classroom environment to determine which materials and resources support the success of DLLs with various abilities.

Adapting Materials for All Children

> Include puzzles with various amounts of pieces, sizes, and textures; for example, you might provide knob puzzles for children with fine motor challenges.

Selecting Inclusive Books for All Children

> Select books such as *Rolling Along with Goldilocks and the Three Bears*, by Cindy Meyers, that provide DLLs with various abilities opportunities to see themselves as the main character of the story.

Summary

DLLs are affected by educators and how they tailor their classroom environment to build on children's background knowledge. Educators of DLLs create print-rich environments where labels, signs, and words are found everywhere, and everyday opportunities abound to build on children's emerging literacy skills. The way we set up our environment sends clear messages to children and families about our philosophy, values, and beliefs. Consider the cultural and linguistic appropriateness of all the classroom areas, including the materials, resources, schedules, and routines, and ensure that all children are valued for their cultural wealth. Now close your eyes and visualize your favorite childhood environment. What made that particular place special? We challenge you to think about the DLLs in your care. Have you created a safe, nurturing space that augments children's learning and development?

Key Points to Remember!

> Understanding and respecting the familial culture of DLLs is crucial in building a foundation for providing an environment that nurtures children's overall well-being. The child's environment includes the content educators arrange in the classroom, the atmosphere they create, and the feeling they communicate within that environment (Gordon & Browne 2017).

> Responsive educators are knowledgeable of children's home languages and cultures and use this knowledge to plan learning environments that support bilingual and bicultural development (Castro, Espinosa, & Páez 2011; Genesee, Paradis, & Crago 2004).

> The resources from home and the community become endless opportunities to develop language and literacy for DLLs.

> It is important for educators to select books, posters, puzzles, toys, and games that represent the cultural diversity of the classroom (Espinosa 2015).

> Consider the language, race, ethnicity, family structure, disabilities, and occupations of the families in your early childhood program.

> Effective teachers thoughtfully plan a print-rich environment where DLLs can playfully explore literacy-enhancing materials, resources, and visuals in two languages (Roskos & Neuman 2001).

> When their environment is predictable, it creates a safe, warm, and engaging classroom that is not dependent on understanding and speaking English (National Center on Cultural and Linguistic Responsiveness 2020).

> DLLs benefit from regular routines that are presented with simple repetitive songs or chants and simple motions or visual cues for transitions.

> A well-prepared environment will ease arrivals and dismissals for DLLs.

Frequently Asked Questions

Why should my classroom environment reflect and include the languages and cultures of DLLs in my classroom?

When educators include environmental print, visuals, books, and materials that reflect children's home languages and cultures, they demonstrate respect for the home languages and cultures of children and their families. It also allows for children and families to read the environment and make connections between English and their home languages. It facilitates learning for DLLs by building on their prior knowledge while helping them feel included.

Where can I find materials or resources that represent the culture and language of DLLs in my classroom?

Educators must collaborate with families of DLLs to support their culture and language. Invite them to donate familiar environmental print and materials from home and their communities to include in the classroom environment and integrate these resources into the daily classroom learning activities. Families bring much cultural wealth..

References

Alanís, I. 2013. "Where's My Partner? Developing Effective Bilingual Pairs for Dual Language Classrooms." *Young Children* 68 (1): 42–47.

Alanís, I., I. Salinas-González, & M. Arreguín-Anderson. 2015. "Developing Biliteracy with Intentional Support: Using Interactive Word Walls and Paired Learning." *Young Children* 70 (4): 46–51.

Arreguín-Anderson, M.G., I. Alanís, & I. Salinas-González. 2016. "Using Acorns to Generate an Entire Alphabet!" *Science and Children* 53 (6): 76–81.

Castro, D.C., L.M. Espinosa, & M. Páez. 2011. "Defining and Measuring Quality in Early Childhood Practices that Promote Dual Language Learners' Development and Learning." In *Quality Measurement in Early Childhood Settings,* eds. M. Zaslow, I. Martinez-Beck, K. Tout, & T. Halle, 257–80. Baltimore: Brookes.

Epstein, A.S. 2014. *The Intentional Teacher: Choosing the Best Strategies for Young Children's Learning.* Rev. ed. Washington, DC: NAEYC; Ypsilanti, MI: HighScope.

Espinosa, L.M. 2015. *Getting It Right for Young Children from Diverse Backgrounds: Applying Research to Improve Practice with a Focus on Dual Language Learners.* 2nd ed. Upper Saddle River, NJ: Pearson Education.

Fountas, I.C., & G.S. Pinnell. 2010. *The Continuum of Literacy Learning, Grades PreK–2: A Guide to Teaching.* 2nd ed. Portsmouth, NH: Heinemann.

García, E. 2003. "Respecting Children's Home Languages and Cultures." In *A World of Difference: Readings on Teaching Young Children in a Diverse Society,* ed. C. Copple. Washington, DC: NAEYC.

García, O., & L. Wei. 2014. *Translanguaging: Language, Bilingualism and Education.* New York: Palgrave Macmillan.

Genesee, F., J. Paradis, & M. Crago. 2004. *Dual Language Development and Disorders: A Handbook on Bilingualism and Second Language Learning.* Baltimore: Brookes.

Gonzalez-Mena, J. 2011. *Foundations of Early Childhood Education: Teaching Children in a Diverse Setting.* 5th ed. New York: McGraw-Hill.

Gonzalez, N., L. Moll, & C. Amanti. 2005. *Funds of Knowledge: Theorizing Practice in Households, Communities and Classrooms.* Mahwah, NJ: Lawrence Erlbaum.

Gordon, A.M., & K.W. Browne. 2017. *Beginnings and Beyond: Foundations in Early Childhood Education.* 10th ed. Boston: Cengage Learning.

IOM (Institute of Medicine) & NRC (National Research Council). 2000. *From Neurons to Neighborhoods: The Science of Early Childhood Development.* Eds. J.P. Shonkoff & D.A. Phillips. Report. Washington, DC: National Academies Press. doi:10.17226/9824.

Love, A., M.S. Burns, & M. Buell. 2007. "Writing: Empowering Literacy." *Young Children* 62 (1): 12–19.

Magruder, E., W. Hayslip, L. Espinosa, & C. Matera. 2013. "Many Languages, One Teacher: Supporting Language and Literacy Development for Preschool Dual Language Learners." *Young Children* 68 (1): 8–15.

Moll, L.C., C. Amanti, D. Neff, & N. Gonzalez. 1992. "Funds of Knowledge for Teaching: Using a Qualitative Approach to Connect Homes and Classrooms." *Theory into Practice* 31 (2): 132–141.

NAEYC. 2019. "Advancing Equity in Early Childhood Education." Position statement. Washington, DC: NAEYC. www.naeyc.org /resources/position-statements/equity.

NASEM (National Academies of Sciences, Engineering, and Medicine). 2017. *Promoting the Educational Success of Children and Youth Learning English: Promising Futures.* Washington, DC: National Academies Press. doi:10.17226/24677.

National Center on Cultural and Linguistic Responsiveness. 2020. Retrieved from https://eclkc.ohs.acf.hhs.gov/culture-language.

National Early Literacy Panel. 2008. *Developing Early Literacy: A Scientific Synthesis of Early Literacy Development and Implications for Intervention.* Washington, DC: National Institute for Literacy.

Roskos, K., & S.B. Neuman. 2001. "The Environment and Its Influences for Early Literacy Teaching and Learning." In *The Handbook of Early Literacy Research,* eds. S.B. Neuman & D.K. Dickinson, 281–94. New York: Guilford Press.

Salinas-González, I., M. Arreguín-Anderson, & I. Alanís. 2015. "Classroom Labels that Young Children Can Use: Enhancing Biliteracy Development in a Dual Language Classroom." *Dimensions of Early Childhood* 43 (1): 25–32.

Tabors, P.O. 2008. *One Child, Two Languages: A Guide for Early Childhood Educators of Children Learning English as a Second Language.* 2nd ed. Baltimore: Brookes.

Yosso, T.J. 2005. "Whose Culture Has Capital? A Critical Race Theory Discussion of Community Cultural Wealth." *Race, Ethnicity, and Education* 8 (1): 69–91.

naeyc® Accreditation
Early Learning Programs

This chapter supports the following NAEYC Early Learning Program Accreditation Standards and Topic Areas:

Standard 1: Relationships

1.A Building Positive Relationships Between Teachers and Families

1.B Building Positive Relationships Between Teachers and Children

1.D Creating a Predictable, Consistent, and Harmonious Classroom

Standard 3: Teaching

3.A Designing Enriched Learning Environments

3.B Creating Caring Communities for Learning

3.D Using Time, Grouping, and Routines to Achieve Learning Goals

3.E Responding to Children's Interests and Needs

3.F Making Learning Meaningful for All Children

5 Understanding and Facilitating Play

Objectives

> Explain the value of play for dual language learners.

> Explore how dual language learners engage in translingual play.

> Examine how dual language learners engage in various types of play.

> Discuss strategies that facilitate guided play.

> Describe how play supports the development of dual language learners with disabilities.

In the preschool classroom at an early childhood center, three children are engaged in the dramatic play center, pretending to buy bread at their local *panadería*. Their teacher joins in the play by saying, "Good morning, sir. I'm delivering the two tongs the manager ordered for his bakery."

Carlos smiles, gets the tongs, and tells the others, *"Pa' garrar el pan."* (To get the bread). Cheerfully, Jorge responds, "Okay, I'm getting the *pan!*" (bread).

Alberto chimes in, *"¡Yo también quiero comprar pan!"* (I want to buy bread too!)

Patty exclaims, *"¡Sí, para la fiesta!"* (Yes, for the party!)

Culturally relevant play experiences are at the heart of appropriate instructional designs for DLLs. In this vignette, DLLs engage in the flexible use of language codes while pretending to buy bread at their local *panadería* (bakery). High-quality, early childhood education programs organize instruction around standards that focus on "understanding young children's characteristics and needs, supporting and engaging families, positive relationships and supportive interactions, and developmentally appropriate teaching" (NAEYC 2020, 7). Included in these standards is the value of play in all children's lives. These playful environments coupled with positive adult and peer relationships contribute to the early learning and language development of DLLs (Espinosa 2015). Early childhood educators understand that diverse experiences and unique languages influence children's development (Castro, Espinosa, & Páez 2011). When these experiences are reflected in play spaces, DLLs make connections and tend to use their full linguistic repertoire, a practice known as **translingual play** (Arreguín-Anderson, Salinas-González, & Alanís 2018). During translingual play, DLLs make sense of the world around them and creatively use language.

In this chapter, we discuss the value of play for DLLs, including DLLs with varying abilities, and how play supports their development. We also cover the types of play DLLs are involved in, including translingual play, along with ways teachers can enhance their language during these types of play. This is followed by practical ways that teachers facilitate language opportunities through guided play.

The Value of Play for Dual Language Learners

There is widespread consensus that play is essential for the healthy development of all children, but it is especially important in the growth and development of DLLs (AAP 2018; Burton & Edwards 2008). High-quality early childhood programs for children from birth to age 5 include adult-supported, play-based learning experiences that assist DLLs as they build a strong foundation for their future learning. DLLs benefit from supportive play-based environments that nurture the development of their languages through positive support of their socioemotional, cognitive, physical, aesthetic, and cultural identity. These areas of children's development intersect and influence children's language development. In this section, we focus on the various ways play enhances and supports children's linguistic development.

Play Creates Context Embedded Learning Opportunities for DLLs

Play provides hands-on experiences with materials that allow DLLs to explore the purpose and structure of language in authentic ways. The opening vignette illustrates an educational setting designed with culturally relevant materials in mind. It demonstrates how children used cues to decipher and interpret language while pretending to buy bread at their local

panadería (bakery). The teacher strategically introduced the tongs as a new prop for their bakery at a moment when she had children's attention (Salinas-González, Arreguín-Anderson, & Alanís 2019). Through their role play, children adopted the term and began to use it within a meaningful context.

Play Creates a Space for DLLs to Engage in Translingual Play

An environment that promotes learning through play establishes an informal, nonthreatening atmosphere where DLLs are more likely to explore and take risks with their language. For example, while playing *panadería* (bakery) in the dramatic play center, Carlos says *"Pa'garrar el pan"* (To get the bread) as he holds the tongs, Jorge cheerfully announces "I'm getting the *pan!* (bread)," and Patty exclaims *"¡Sí para la fiesta!"* (Yes, for the party!). Their culturally relevant dramatic play center provides a level of comfort where children translanguage, or alternate language codes for meaningful purposes to communicate without concern about adhering to a prescribed language.

During translingual play, DLLs use "multimodal gestures, objects, visual cues, touch, sounds, and other modes of communication besides words" to enable play to work (García & Wei, 2014, 28). In other words, children are motivated to communicate intentionally to regulate the course of action of their play frames. For example, while playing to be at the *panadería,* children often imitate sounds and gestures in their environment, such as "ping!" to communicate to other players that the bread is ready in the oven and waving their hand at other children to come and buy some bread.

Children use translanguaging to regulate each other's behaviors during play, signal they are ready to leave the play episode, transition to a new play episode, express commands, perform an action, or tell someone to perform an action (Bengochea, Sembiante, & Gort 2018). For example, as 5-year-old children play in their sociodramatic play center, Tomas might announce, "Let's play groceries!" as he transitions his playmates to the new play episode. Marisa exclaims, "Okay, *yo vendo y tú compras.*" (Okay, I'll sell and you buy.) "Okay, yes?" Marisa uses Spanish to inform the players of their actions but then used English to confirm their agreement. As DLLs play, they freely adjust and practice their languages. They learn to use various strategies to communicate and interact with other children (Arreguín-Anderson, Salinas-González, & Alanís 2018). Within this space, children understand they have the freedom to use whatever language they have without fear of correction from their teachers.

DLLs Engage in All Types of Play

Play is universal and has no cultural boundaries. It reflects children's cultural experiences and may take many forms. There is a general sequence to the development of social play for children. This sequence, however, may look differently for DLLs who are in a new environment where a different language is used by their teachers and peers. DLLs display a variety of play behaviors depending on their social comfort level with themselves, others, and their environment, and may not necessarily follow predetermined stages of patterns based on Euro-American cultural patterns. Understanding the social levels of play helps educators recognize children's social values, family practices, and individual interests. Let's explore the many ways DLLs engage in play.

DLLs may engage in **onlooker play** as they observe other children play. They may talk to themselves or others but will not enter the play episode of others. Sometimes, DLLs may be reluctant or unsure of how to enter into play. At other times, they may be figuring out which play activity to select or the proper word labels to use, or they may simply be interested in how others play. Once they are ready, they will join the play. Sensitive teachers understand children's onlooking behavior as part of the play continuum. They observe DLLs skillfully to determine if they need help in making choices about their play, need language support, or if they are simply learning to play through observation.

---

onlooker play
Children observing other children play.

solitary play
Children playing alone with toys or object.

parallel play
Children playing alongside other children without interacting with each other.

associative play
Children using the same materials during play and socially interacting with each other but without a common play theme.

linguistic or language scaffold
Language support provided by adults that encourage children to interact.

Although **solitary play** is often typical for infants and toddlers, sometimes older DLLs play alone even though other children may be present. They may need time to explore on their own or may need to get away from excessive stimulation from the new language, other children, or their new environment. You may worry that children are being left out of the social play with others. However, assess the situation before encouraging children to participate in group play. DLLs need both opportunities to play by themselves and opportunities to play with others as they adjust to their new environment.

During **parallel play,** children play alongside others but without interacting with each other. It is common to see toddlers involved in parallel play as they are becoming aware of others. However, older DLLs might also engage in parallel play. For example, a young DLL may sit next to other children in the block center and share the blocks but not get involved with others' play. They may also use nonverbal negotiation of materials but have no connection to other children's play. As children learn how to play with others in a new culture and language, they may also imitate each other's actions or gestures during parallel play. Playing next to others is a gradual way for DLLs to work their way into a group during play episodes. As their ability to socialize with others increases, they will display the next two types of social play, which are typical of preschoolers and older children. Again, remember that children develop at different rates and their familial experiences enhance their development.

Associative play involves children using the same materials during play and socially interacting with each other. However, this type of play is not organized or planned. Children may be finger painting at the art center and interacting sporadically about the paint colors used but continue to paint on their own. Educators can support the language development of DLLs during this type of play through **linguistic or language scaffolding** as they interact with children (Otto 2018). The following example demonstrates how educators attentively observe to provide appropriate support that encourages children's verbal participation through the use of questioning, expansion, and repetition:

Ms. Lee, the kindergarten teacher, has been observing Cara and Kim playing in the block center. They occasionally borrow blocks from one another, but their verbal exchanges are limited and they are not working together to create structures. Ms. Lee sits with them on the rug and says, "Hi, Cara and Kim. I see that you have been building something very tall." Cara responds, "Hi, Ms. Lee," and Kim says, "Hi, it is a building." Cara corrects her by saying, "No, mine is a tall apartment." Ms. Lee attempts to combine the two responses. "Oh, so Kim is constructing a building and Cara is constructing a tall apartment." Kim adds, "Mine is also a tall apartment." Ms. Lee extends their ideas by asking, "Who lives in these tall apartments?" Cara answers, "I'm going to live here and Kim will live there. Okay?" Kim agrees. Ms. Lee says, "That sounds like a great plan!"

Ms. Lee encouraged both girls to play together and to talk about their play plan. Effective educators ask children about what they are doing, expand on what the children have said during their play, and use repetition to clarify what they have said (Otto 2018).

On the other hand, **cooperative play** involves complex efforts to organize play. Children may negotiate play themes, their roles, and their constructions.

In Mrs. Espinosa's bilingual prekindergarten classroom, four girls are in the dramatic play center. Ana, Yolanda, Sonia, and Viola engage in coordinating their role play.

· · ·

Ana: Let's play *a la cocinita*! (Let's play we're at the kitchen!) You be the mommy and I'll be the baby.

Yolanda: *Quien va ser la abuelita* to cook for us? (Who will be the grandma to cook for us?)

Sonia: I'll be *abuelita* (grandma). Let's pretend *abuelita* burned the tortillas and we call the fire truck.

Viola: (*Watches the other girls, then giggles and runs off to another center.*)

Sometimes DLLs, such as Viola, may participate in onlooker play, finding it challenging to participate fully in cooperative play, particularly when the other children in the group are not speaking their native language. Families have identified that their bilingual children will observe others playing before participating with their peers (Michael-Luna 2013). Therefore, they may need the time to observe play behaviors or understand the play language being used before they feel comfortable to gradually join others during play. Understanding the various ways DLLs play is important because it helps educators support children's daily play while enhancing their language development (Alanís & Arreguín-Anderson 2015).

cooperative play
Involves complex efforts to organize a common play theme.

Playing with Familial Literacy Stationery

› Ask families to donate old greeting cards, stationery, or postcards to encourage children to emulate meaningful family literacy events (e.g., making a grocery list, writing a letter to a relative) at the dramatic play center or the writing center.

Facilitating Guided Play for DLLs

Early childhood educators support play by setting up the learning environment, gathering play materials, and including play in their daily schedule. They observe DLLs while they play to determine what interests them and to learn about their individual variations in learning. They also act as a resource and interact with children when needed. DLLs benefit from educators who know when to join children at play and when to remain outside their play activity. If adults interrupt children's play, the flow of play may be influenced and children may change it to please others. When DLLs encounter challenging play opportunities, the educator should provide scaffolding by asking the right questions or providing the needed resources to guide children's outcomes.

Strategies to Guide Play of DLLs

In this section, we provide three strategies that provide support and guide children's play (Salinas-González, Arreguín-Anderson, & Alanís 2019).

1. **Spark conversations during play through verbal mapping.** Describe to children what they are doing or the objects they are playing with in meaningful contexts. As discussed in Chapter 3, representational language includes labels for objects and actions that are at the center of children's attention.

2. **Provide new props to extend children's play in three phases.** Educators have a critical role in organizing their environment to maximize everyone's participation in play. Equip the play areas (e.g., math, dramatic play, construction) with objects, props, and literacy materials in gradual phases to build on their knowledge and extend their play interest. Figure 5.1 reflects each phase during a flea market play theme.

3. **Create a print-rich play environment.** Include functional labels, pictures, books, and other materials reflective of children's culture and language. This will encourage DLLs to be involved in emergent literacy activities while they play.

Building with Familial Boxes

› Encourage families to donate a variety of hollow boxes (e.g., food, storage, shoes) for children to explore in the construction center.

› As children explore the boxes, narrate their actions by saying things like "You are placing all the bigger boxes on the bottom," or "I see you have used five boxes for your creation."

Imagining with Pashminas or Towels

› Provide a variety of *rebozos* (shawls) or pashminas in the dramatic play center for children to engage in open-ended, culturally relevant, and imaginative roles. Towels work great too!

› Depending on their experiences, children may use the rebozos as a dress or to carry babies on their back. You may even see superheroes or *luchadores* (wrestlers) wearing their rebozos as capes.

Phase 1	Phase 2	Phase 3
Provide basic objects, props, and materials related to the play theme	Add more resources based on careful observation of children's play interactions and discussions during the play theme.	When interest in a play theme is fading, add more complex resources to enhance and extend children's imaginations.
Example: Supply clothing, shoes, money, toys, and writing materials for children to pretend buying and selling at the flea market.	Example: After hearing children talk about buying food at their local flea market, pretend corn, corn toppings, snow cones, and flavorings can be added.	Example: Adding a police hat and a firefighter hat extends children's play into finding lost children, saving people, and directing traffic at the flea market.

Figure 5.1. Introduction of props in sociodramatic play areas.

Play Supports DLLs with Disabilities

DLLs diagnosed with a disability or delay benefit from participating in early childhood settings that promote inclusive play-based environments (Barton & Wolery 2010). Depending on the age of the child, an **Individualized Family Service Plan (IFSP)** for children who are younger than 3 years old or an **Individualized Education Plan (IEP)** for children who are 3 years old and above will "regularly include play as a way to acquire required social, cognition, language, and motor skills and competencies" (Sluss 2015, 243). An ESL specialist may work together with the special education teacher to provide appropriate supports and services for DLLs.

DLLs have varying abilities and special needs in both languages. Thus, they benefit from supportive playful environments that validate their home language(s) while developing their second language (Gutiérrez-Clellen, Simon-Cereijido, & Sweet 2012). Too often, educators have the misconception that children with a disability or developmental delay need to be involved in direct instruction learning skills rather than playing with other children (Hanline & Daley 2002). Play, however, provides a natural context for engaging DLLs in individual and social play. It increases their engagement and promotes interactions with others. Intentional planning that uses children's preferences for play moves them toward successful **inclusion** in the dual

Individualized Family Service Plan (IFSP)
Written plan that guides the early intervention process and services for a child younger than 3 years old and his family.

Individualized Education Plan (IEP)
Written plan that outlines the learning goals of a child with a disability (3 years old and above) and the services to be provided to meet that child's educational needs.

inclusion
Educating children with disabilities and children without disabilities together in the same learning environment.

Creating Literacy Spaces During Play

› Include dry-erase markers and a laminated three-by-three-foot piece of butcher paper stapled or taped to the wall to serve as a literacy wall that children may adapt to the changing play theme.

› If you do not have wall space, laminated blank pieces of paper are also great literacy tools.

Adapting Painting Opportunities

› Make a hole in a tennis ball and insert art tools such as crayons, markers, or a small pastry brush to allow children with various abilities to grip the tools while playing in the art center.

language setting (Catlett & Soukakou 2019). Consider the following suggestions when organizing learning through play for DLLs with varying abilities:

› Provide both home language and second language support.

› Adapt play materials to meet children's individual needs and interests.

› Support their active play with a visual activity map that can focus children on steps of an activity (Catlett & Soukakou 2019).

› Model play-based activities to encourage involvement.

› Pair children to help others engage in play activities and develop prosocial behaviors.

Summary

It is important to be keen observers of all children in your care in order to provide an engaging learning environment that is responsive to their needs. Engaging learning environments for DLLs include play experiences tailored to children's developmental needs while also including culture and language(s). In this chapter, we provided various examples of how DLLs engage in play, focusing on their linguistic and social levels while providing them with linguistic support. Understanding the language and culture of DLLs is a crucial component of environments that engage them and challenge their individual abilities. Educators need to be sensitive to the socioemotional, cultural, and linguistic experiences that influence the play of DLLs. This will ensure DLLs feel valued within a comfortable, safe learning environment that promotes their use of language within a meaningful context.

Key Points to Remember!

› DLLs benefit from supportive play-based environments that nurture the development of their languages through positive support of their socioemotional, cognitive, physical, aesthetic, and cultural identity.

› Play provides hands-on experiences with materials that allow DLLs to explore the purpose and structure of language in authentic ways and promotes an informal, nonthreatening atmosphere in which DLLs are more likely to explore and take risks with their language.

› During translingual play, DLLs use "multimodal gestures, objects, visual cues, touch, sounds, and other modes of communication besides words" to enable play to work (García & Wei 2014, 28).

› Children use translanguaging to regulate each other's behaviors during play, signal they are ready to leave the play episode, transition to a new play episode, express commands, perform an action, or tell someone to perform an action (Bengochea, Sembiante, & Gort 2018).

> DLLs display a variety of play behaviors depending on their social comfort level with themselves, others, and their environment, and may not necessarily follow predetermined stages of patterns based on Euro-American cultural patterns.

> DLLs need both opportunities to play by themselves and opportunities to play with others as they adjust to their new environment.

> Support play by setting up the learning environment, gathering play materials, and including play in the daily schedule. Observe DLLs while they play to determine what interests them and to learn about their individual variations in learning.

> DLLs have varying abilities and special needs in both languages.

Frequently Asked Questions

How can my classroom environment engage DLLs in playful learning?

A warm and nurturing environment that reflects children's home language and culture invites DLLs to participate and learn. Include books, toys, songs, games, and print materials that reflect children's cultures and home languages. Listen to children's voices during play, incorporate their ideas into the play centers and play themes. It sends them a clear message that they are valued and respected as learners.

In what language should I engage the children during play?

Even when the language of instruction is English, teachers should continue to provide opportunities for DLLs to develop their home language during play. Play is a motivating activity. It provides many opportunities for language learning in meaningful social interactions with educators and peers. Allow children to use language freely during play. This will promote richer conversations or connections among children. The educator may continue to expose children to English while children play.

References

Alanís, I., & M. Arreguín-Anderson. 2015. "Developing Paired Learning in Dual Language Classrooms." *Early Years: Journal of the Texas Association for the Education of Young Children* 36 (1): 24–28.

AAP (American Academy of Pediatrics). 2018. "The Power of Play: A Pediatric Role in Enhancing Development in Young Children." *Pediatrics* 142 (3): 1–12.

Arreguín-Anderson, M., I. Salinas-González, & I. Alanís. 2018. "Translingual Play that Promotes Cultural Connections, Invention, and Regulation: A LatCrit Perspective." *International Multilingual Research Journal* 12 (4): 273–87.

Barton, E.E., & M. Wolery. 2010. "Training Teachers to Promote Pretend Play in Young Children with Disabilities." *Exceptional Children* 77 (1): 85–106.

Bengochea, A., S.F. Sembiante, & M. Gort. 2018. "An Emergent Bilingual Child's Multimodal Choices in Sociodramatic Play." *Journal of Early Childhood Literacy* 18 (1): 38–70.

Burton, S.J., & L.C. Edwards. 2008. "Creative Play: Building Connections with Children Who Are Learning English." *Annual Editions: Early Childhood Education* 29: 60–65.

Castro, D.C., L.M. Espinosa, & M. Páez. 2011. "Defining and Measuring Quality in Early Childhood Practices that Promote Dual Language

Learners' Development and Learning." In *Quality Measurement in Early Childhood Settings,* eds. M. Zaslow, I. Martinez-Beck, K. Tout, & T. Halle, 257–80. Baltimore: Brookes.

Catlett, C., & E.P. Soukakou. 2019. "Assessing Opportunities to Support Each Child: 12 Practices for Quality Inclusion." *Young Children* 74 (3): 34–43.

Espinosa, L.M. 2015. *Getting It Right for Young Children from Diverse Backgrounds: Applying Research to Improve Practice with a Focus on Dual Language Learners.* 2nd ed. Upper Saddle River, NJ: Pearson Education.

García, O., & L. Wei. 2014. *Translanguaging: Language, Bilingualism, and Education.* New York: Palgrave Macmillan.

Gutiérrez-Clellen, V., G. Simon-Cereijido, & M. Sweet. 2012. "Predictors of Second Language Acquisition in Latino Children with Specific Language Impairment." *American Journal of Speech-Language Pathology* 21 (1): 64–77.

Hanline, M.F., & S. Daley. 2002. "'Mom, Will Kaelie Always Have Possibilities?' The Realities of Early Childhood Inclusion." *Phi Delta Kappan* 84 (1): 73–76.

Michael-Luna, S. 2013. "What Linguistically Diverse Parents Know and How It Can Help Early Childhood Educators: A Case Study of a Dual Language Preschool Community." *Early Childhood Education Journal* 41 (6): 447–455.

NAEYC. 2020. "Professional Standards and Competencies for Early Childhood Educators." Position statement. Washington, DC: NAEYC. www.naeyc.org/sites/default/files/globally -shared/downloads/PDFs/resources/position -statements/professional_standards_and _competencies_for_early_childhood _educators.pdf.

Otto, B. 2018. *Language Development in Early Childhood.* Upper Saddle River, NJ: Pearson.

Salinas González, I., M.G. Arreguín-Anderson, & I. Alanís. 2018. "Supporting Language: Culturally Rich Dramatic Play." *Teaching Young Children* 11 (2): 4–6.

Sluss, D.J. 2015. *Supporting Play in Early Childhood: Environment, Curriculum, Assessment.* 2nd ed. Stamford, CT: Cengage Learning.

This chapter supports the following NAEYC Early Learning Program Accreditation Standards and Topic Areas:

Standard 1: Relationships
1.B Building Positive Relationships Between Teachers and Children
1.C Helping Children Make Friends

Standard 2: Curriculum
2.A Essential Characteristics
2.B Social and Emotional Development
2.C Physical Development

2.D Language Development
2.J Creative Expression and Appreciation for the Arts

Standard 3: Teaching
3.A Designing Enriched Learning Environments
3.B Creating Caring Communities for Learning
3.E Responding to Children's Interests and Needs
3.F Making Learning Meaningful for All Children

6 Developing Bilingualism and Biliteracy Across the Content Areas

Objectives

> Discuss the role of all language skills in biliteracy development.

> Examine an interdisciplinary inquiry approach for biliteracy development across the content areas.

> Analyze strategies that promote biliteracy in a dual language classroom.

Carmen is a very active and talkative bilingual child who started attending prekindergarten in a local dual language school. Carmen's teacher, Ms. López, is not sure about the best way to continue fostering Carmen's bilingualism and biliteracy, so she asked her colleague, Ms. Zavala, for suggestions. As they talked, Ms. Zavala shared ideas for promoting language development across the content areas, including a learning sequence that begins with hands-on activities and partner-based learning strategies that she learned at a recent professional development session. Ms. Zavala explained how the suggested techniques would allow Ms. Lopez to scaffold all children's learning as they continue developing their biliteracy skills.

In numerous settings across the country, young children just like Carmen have the potential to maintain their home language while becoming bilingual and biliterate. As discussed in Chapter 2, many children who grow up as simultaneous or sequential bilinguals often acquire vocabulary in one language and a different set of concepts in another language. Depending on contextual factors, such as the programs in place in the centers or schools that they attend, bilingual preschoolers may or may not continue to develop both languages socially or academically.

When not provided with the support to develop literacy skills in their home language, emergent bilingual children will often maintain the skills to communicate orally, but they may not necessarily become biliterate. Worse, they may experience considerable difficulty reading and writing in either or both languages. Understanding how dual language learners acquire knowledge of two languages will enable you to support their path toward bilingualism and biliteracy. It will also inform your choices regarding methods and strategies that integrate all language skills, including listening, speaking, reading, and writing in interconnected ways (Soltero-González & Reyes 2012). This chapter will discuss the topics of biliteracy development and an integrated approach to language and content learning. Additionally, we highlight strategies to support children's continuous growth in two languages.

Biliteracy Development of DLLs

As an educator in an early childhood dual language classroom, you may have noticed that young children easily engage in activities that involve active exploration and play. This reminds us that in order to develop literacy skills in two languages, educators should create responsive and enticing contexts in which children can seamlessly engage in motivating and developmentally appropriate tasks that integrate all language skills while relating to concepts in all content areas (Konishi et al. 2014). We know that development of a first or second language follows similar patterns. Children initially develop receptive language (listening), and then they acquire mastery and knowledge of oral language skills (speaking). Finally, children learn to read and write, as explained in the following section (Otto 2018).

Listening and Speaking

Listening skills of DLLs are enhanced when they listen to adults who produce rich, precise language to name objects, describe actions, and explain events in patterns of interaction that involve them. This exposure to quality language along with opportunities to speak will equip young DLLs with skills needed to later engage in reading with comprehension and to work through barriers that may arise when they encounter complex vocabulary.

oracy
The ability to express oneself through oral language. The development of oral skills includes children's ability to engage in meaningful literacy related discussions, command of complex grammar; and use of meaningful vocabulary in context (Escamilla et al. 2014).

In a dual language classroom, **oracy** (listening and speaking) objectives should be different for each language (Escamilla et al. 2014). What do we mean? In many cases, bilingual children's speaking skills may be stronger in Spanish. Therefore, one might expect Spanish oracy objectives to be slightly more advanced than English oracy objectives. In other words, what we expect children to accomplish in their home languages will be at a higher level.

Oracy objectives in English and children's home languages include:

> Listening and speaking objectives in English: Children will listen to a story and retell it using complete sentences.

> Listening and speaking objectives in children's home languages: Children will listen to a story and retell it using sentence stems that signal a sequence (e.g., *first, next, then, finally*).

When planning speaking and listening activities for DLLs, connections to previous knowledge are likely to promote active involvement while enhancing their existing skills. Keep in mind that, in general, oracy instruction should engage children in opportunities to speak for varied purposes, including describing what they know or see, explaining their understanding of new experiences, narrating a sequence of events, retelling stories, singing songs related to those stories and experiences, and expressing their learning.

Emergent Reading and Writing

Support for children's home languages is essential, and we know that the literacy skills that children acquire in their first language will transfer to their second language and vice versa, thus facilitating development of reading and writing skills in both languages (Goldenberg 2013). Reading instruction in dual language classrooms should be strategically planned in each language. Table 6.1 shows recommended practices in a dual language classroom in which most young learners speak a language other than English at home.

Writing tasks should be connected to ongoing reading lessons to enhance young learners' ability to identify sound–symbol relationships (phonics) and other aspects of language knowledge. Two critical elements in emergent writing engagement include a continuously scaffolded process that emphasizes modeled writing through a language experience approach and independent writing (Escamilla et al. 2014).

Additionally, opportunities for independent writing and drawing as part of a meaningful task allow children to develop ownership. Initially, unconventional writing dominates children's production regardless of language dominance. Once children are ready and regardless of

Creating Opportunities to Promote Oracy

> After reading a book, provide toy phones to pretend retelling the story to a partner. First model, then invite children to do the same.

> Before walking to the cafeteria or playground, ask for volunteers to tell you what the steps are in order to complete a task (e.g., What are the different things we do at the cafeteria? What are the steps we take to have a good time at the playground?).

Table 6.1. Biliteracy Development in a Dual Language Classroom: Recommended Practices

Language Arts Instruction in Children's Home Languages	Language Arts Instruction in English
> Use culturally relevant texts to establish connections with previous knowledge (in both languages). > Dedicate longer periods of time to literacy instruction in children's home language. > Adopt reading instruction methods aligned with the structure of children's home language. For example, in Spanish, emphasize the syllabic nature of the words as you read to and with children; stress the role of vowels in the process of reading and writing.	> English literacy should connect to topics and skills covered during children's home language literacy instruction. > Ask questions and highlight vocabulary in English as it relates to concepts learned during reading instruction in the home language. > Use books rich in visuals and context clues.

In both cases:

> Model reading for pleasure.

> Connect reading to writing tasks to enhance comprehension and place children in a position in which they can apply knowledge and skills.

Language Experience Approach

The language experience approach combines listening, speaking, reading, and writing and has been used to promote meaningful connections with all language skills.

1. Children participate in hands-on activities or direct experiences as a class.

2. Children take turns in a whole group discussion where they re-create the experience while the teacher transcribes.

3. Teacher and children read and make corrections, changes, and revisions to written text.

4. Children read newly written text chorally, in pairs, and individually.

5. Teacher uses text to extend discussion in subsequent lessons.

This approach illustrates multiple aspects of the writing and reading process. Initially, children see object-symbol-sound connections and ways in which written language conveys a message related to authentic experiences.

language of instruction, young bilingual learners are likely to engage in hybrid literacy practices—that is, they use both languages in discussions with peers or other adults. For example, they may:

> Use their first language as a resource to discuss what they want to express in their drawings or writings in English.

> Use the English language to write or draw about concepts learned in English even during home language instruction.

> Use both languages, or codeswitch, as they discuss what they will write and as they write.

An Interdisciplinary Inquiry Approach for Biliteracy Development Across the Content Areas

At the heart of a developmentally appropriate biliteracy approach is the idea that reading, writing, speaking, and listening are acquired in interconnected ways across the content areas (Beeman & Urow 2013). We also know that young children are better equipped to understand the world around them when they seek answers to their own questions through an inquiry approach (Contant et al. 2018). In their daily lives, young children experience life and events through active exploration. In doing so, they are inclined to speak as they observe, to sing while they play, and to wonder while they use their senses.

Young children benefit from experiences that integrate content and literacy and that advance from concrete to abstract (Kostelnik, Soderman, & Whiren 2011). In the following section, we suggest an interdisciplinary sequence of learning that begins with concrete experiences and actively involves learners in the process of biliteracy development through an inquiry approach. This sequence involves a gradual exposure to writing through a language experience approach followed by an interactive read-aloud to access more abstract aspects of language (see Figure 6.1).

Phase 1: Direct Experiences to Promote Vocabulary Development Through Listening and Speaking

Direct and concrete experiences allow the teacher and children to contextualize language with something tangible. Phase 1 establishes a common understanding of a concept or idea using concrete objects and shared experiences or activities. This common understanding can be used for later discussions related to science, mathematics, social studies, and language arts when concrete objects are no longer within reach. Biliteracy development is an interdisciplinary process because topics that draw children's interest are likely to connect to most content areas, making it easy to introduce rich descriptive vocabulary and relevant concepts, as shown in Figure 6.2.

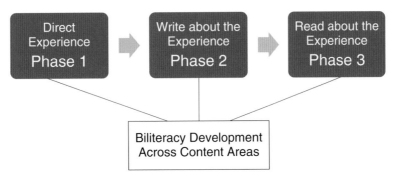

Figure 6.1. Interdisciplinary biliteracy sequence.

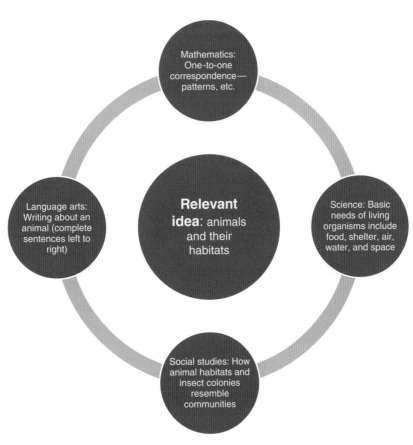

Figure 6.2. Interdisciplinary connection to content areas.

Although we often associate direct experiences or hands-on activities with guided practice or a phase of a lesson that follows an explanation from the teacher, we know that for young children, reversing the order makes more sense; in other words, lessons are more effective when they begin with opportunities to actively explore and construct meaning while gradually removing contextual support (Kostelnik, Soderman, Whiren, & Rupiper 2019). This sequence is beneficial for DLLs because spoken language automatically becomes more comprehensible when it is produced in relation to actions, events, or objects that are at the center of the child's attention (Beeman & Urow 2013; NASEM 2017).

It is during the initial exploration phase of the sequence that you can begin making connections to other content areas by guiding children's inquiry through purposeful questioning, as illustrated in the following scenario:

> Mr. Velez leads his class through an investigation of the school garden. As they begin exploring, he engages in a series of comments and questions that help children connect what they are seeing, hearing, and touching to other areas of the curriculum. He invites children to take a look at insects that live in our garden (connection to science and social studies). He comments, "I wonder where we can find them," and then asks, "Where do you think we should observe?" (connection to science). When Carmen and Jaime find a roly-poly, he says, "I see that you found a roly-poly!" He picks it up for children to see how it turns into a ball. He then asks, "I wonder what it eats and what it uses for shelter" (connection to science). When another group of children point out a spider, he says, "Wow! You discovered a spider. Let's see how many legs it has by counting them" (connection to mathematics). He then adds, "What can we do to help the spider so that it continues eating insects that we don't like?" (connection to social studies).

During Phase 1, Mr. Velez's focus was on developing children's oral language through listening and speaking. At the same time, he helped children make connections to other content areas.

Phase 2: Writing or Drawing About the Hands-on Experience

Biliteracy development involves integration of listening, speaking, writing, and reading in connected ways. Now that children had the opportunity to actively explore, Mr. Velez will tap into this experiential knowledge to introduce big ideas as expressed in the learning objectives. In this case, with his guidance, children will narrate and explain what they saw, touched, smelled, and possibly heard while Mr. Velez writes their responses on chart paper.

To establish a sense of agency in language production, children should immediately engage in writing or drawing activities through a language experience approach or shared writing activity. This phase allows children to see the connection between spoken and written words. In a dual language classroom, this should occur in the child's home language. This shared writing activity lends itself to capturing new words in the form of a class-generated narrative as well as a word wall that can be constructed simultaneously as words emerge during the whole group discussion.

Whole group discussions significantly enhance the possibilities to expand language knowledge in relation to a word because children have firsthand knowledge of that word or concept. For example, as Mr. Velez writes children's ideas and narratives about their trip to the garden, words like *spider* will emerge. Mr. Velez will pause and add these words to the word wall with a pictorial representation when possible. Given that the word *spider* has captured children's attention, he can use that word to generate additional vocabulary associated with spiders, such as *minuscule, legs, arachnid, abdomen,* and *spiderweb*. In doing so, he maintains his initial focus on animals and their habitats, while validating children's observations and increasing vocabulary acquisition. Including these words on a word wall will serve as a useful tool to continue conversations throughout the week.

Phase 3: Read-Alouds to Facilitate Symbolic Experience in a Dual Language Classroom

In Phases 1 and 2, children had direct access to objects, organisms, or places within their garden. They also had the opportunity to listen and talk about them with their peers and with the teacher. Additionally, they translated their experience into a narrated written message connected to a word wall. In Phase 3, children are ready to apply this knowledge by discussing it in different contexts.

Interactive read-alouds should connect to background knowledge in two ways: (1) by relating to the hands-on concrete experience, and (2) by selecting books that closely reflect children's lives. When selecting texts for a read-aloud, it is important to keep in mind that interdisciplinary learning entails sharing books from a variety of genres, including fiction and nonfiction. In science and social studies, for example, informational texts in which connections are made to specific science concepts are critical.

A science informational text will allow DLLs to continue learning science vocabulary and complex language. Ideally, some of the previously discussed words are mentioned in

Identifying Connections in Two Content Areas

> Take small steps. When guiding children during Phase 1, make purposeful connections to at least two content areas. Science and mathematics go hand in hand.

> A question that focuses on close observations can usually be quantified. For example, "Let's take a look at the spots on the twig you found" (connection to science). "How big are they?" (connection to mathematics).

Using Word Walls to Develop Vocabulary

> Strategically place your word wall very close to the space in which you record children's narrative as they tell a story. This will facilitate access as novel words emerge.

> Have index cards and markers in a small tray next to you so that capturing novel vocabulary becomes an easy routine.

Preparing to Address a Relevant Idea in Two Languages

> Plan ahead and identify texts in Spanish and English related to the topic of habitats.

> Having books related to the topic in both languages allows the teacher and children to continue expanding the discussion during any part of the day, even when it is time to change language of instruction.

the selected texts, but there will also be other words that relate to that content and amplify children's conceptual understanding (Hoffman, Collins, & Schickedanz 2015). In sum, informational text provides

> Rich language with lesser-known (i.e., rarer) vocabulary related to the concept of focus

> Inclusion of complex sentence structures (e.g., showing relationships between ideas using words such as *because, since, when*)

An interdisciplinary sequence of learning gradually builds language and content mastery. Initially, the goal is to capitalize on children's inclination to explore with their senses. Active discovery prepares all learners to make connections between print and objects, concepts, or events they have experienced firsthand. Writing and reading about familiar topics facilitates further discussions and connections that expand children's learning.

Strategies to Develop Biliteracy

Meaningful learning promotes biliteracy development because knowledge and language skills (i.e., listening, speaking, reading, and writing) are integrated in purposeful ways. Several strategies support educators as they intentionally promote language development across two language systems, including translingual partner strategies, the creation of child-generated word walls, and oracy through songs, rhymes, or riddles.

Translingual Partner Strategies

Initial exploration activities, shared writing activities, and read-alouds all use interactive approaches in an early childhood classroom. Small groups or pairs in which the teacher includes speakers with different language backgrounds represents a strategy that allows young children to problem solve together while acquiring language skills (Alanís 2013; Rivas 2015). Initially, it is important to encourage social interactions gradually so that children learn the prerequisite skills of turn taking and eye contact. As children develop the necessary skills to engage in partner-based learning, they will tend to use those skills along with a variety of meaning-making tools to accomplish academic tasks. (For strategies to enhance social competence, see Arreguín-Anderson & Alanís 2019.)

When engaged with peers, DLLs use many resources and modes of communication (e.g., oral, written) to construct and convey meaning; therefore, we refer to them as *multimodal learners*. Language is only one resource among many that children use to express themselves or understand others. Canagarajah (2013) identifies other resources, including symbols, icons, images, gestures, tone of voice, and body language. She refers to these as *semiotic resources* because they all help construct and communicate meaning for the learner.

DLLs benefit from instructional practices that extend beyond linguistic resources and specific language modes (such as written language). Multimodal teaching invites children to engage in multiple forms of representation of concepts and ideas (Stein 2008). To convey the idea of *smooth* and *rough,* for example, a multimodal teacher combines the knowledge of developmentally appropriate practices with linguistically responsive strategies to design a complete language experience. Initially, children would use their senses to explore the texture of an assortment of materials. Then they would apply knowledge acquired through this initial exposure to other settings. For instance, they would participate in partner-based discussions with the goal of identifying and classifying objects as rough or smooth. Finally, children would use drawings to illustrate their reasoning, thus employing several modes of representation.

Translingual partner discussions can be more effective when teachers assign partners based on a language inventory conducted at the beginning of the school year. A language inventory will reveal the array of languages present in the classroom, but it should also allow the teacher to map language varieties (standard English, Mexican Spanish, TexMex, Spanglish, Chicano Spanish) and language skills (listening, speaking, reading, and writing). This inventory should inform daily grouping and pairing decisions. (For more information on the development of language inventories, see Arreguín-Anderson & Alanís 2019.) For example, when Mr. Velez's class visited the school garden, knowledge of children's language practices would be useful in deciding how to pair children.

In a hypothetical scenario, a language inventory may reveal that 10 children in his classroom are Spanish dominant, while 10 children are English dominant. This scenario can be further analyzed as we design interactive activities (e.g., interest stations, learning centers, circle time conversations) as illustrated in Table 6.2.

Knowing children linguistically is key when creating opportunities for them to talk with each other. For their trip to the garden, Carmen and Jaime, for instance, would be an ideal pair to promote language acquisition and vocabulary development. While exploring insects together, Carmen may pick up the magnifying lens and tell Jaime, "Look at this roly-poly! Its body is gray!" In this simple interaction, Jaime is learning vocabulary, syntactic features of language, and science content from Carmen. Table 6.3 shows the progression in children's interactive skills.

Table 6.2. Language Inventory in a Linguistically Diverse Classroom

Child	Language	Language Variants
Jaime	Spanish dominant	Puerto Rican Spanish
Ana	Spanish dominant	North Mexican Spanish
Ernest	Spanish dominant	Guatemalan Spanish
Javier	English dominant	Standard English, Standard Spanish, TexMex
Janie	English dominant	Social English
Carmen	English dominant	Social English

Table 6.3. Partner-Based Learning by Age

Age Group	Appropriate Interactive Practices to Promote Language Development in Pairs
3- to 5-year-olds	Interactions become less self-centered and more complex as children share common goals in pairs: take on specific roles, give and receive help, and give and provide explanations. **What this means in practice:** Because children gradually increase the number of conversational turns as well as their ability to focus on a topic, preschoolers are ready to participate in semi-structured, partner-based interactions related to simple projects and shared tasks (Otto 2018). **Example:** **Teacher:** Tell your partner about your favorite insect and why you like it. Then draw your insect and describe it to your partner.

Child-Generated Word Walls to Develop Biliteracy

The biliteracy sequence of learning presented in this chapter emphasizes vocabulary acquisition related to concepts that children have actually experienced through their senses (e.g., the walk in the garden). This direct approach will be critical to the development of word walls populated with words that hold actual meaning for the children. With this in mind, we suggest the following guidelines in relation to word walls in a dual language classroom:

1. Create a word wall for each language of instruction
   (e.g., one in English and one in Spanish).

2. Only add words that relate to firsthand experiences children have had in the context of class discussions. This will allow children to identify meaning and make connections to previous knowledge.

3. Remove words that children already know and place them in a learning center for further use.

4. Add words in the language of instruction (e.g., during Spanish read-aloud discussions, add to the Spanish word wall; during English read-aloud discussions, add to the English word wall). The same word does not need to be translated to the other word wall.

5. Use a generative approach. For example, when discussing spiders, Mr. Velez can point out that spiders make a web, have eight legs, spin webs, and have an abdomen. He can add all four words to the English word wall.

Oracy Through Riddles, Rhymes, and Songs

We propose that biliteracy initiatives connect directly with children's cultural experiences, allowing DLLs to gradually discover the playful aspects of language. For Spanish-speaking DLLs, *adivinanzas* (riddles), *rimas* (rhymes), and *canciones* (songs) represent fun ways to explore pragmatic aspects of language (Arreguín-Anderson & Ruiz-Escalante 2015). For children whose receptive language is gradually building, exposure to riddles, rhymes, and songs during the interdisciplinary biliteracy sequence presented earlier in this chapter can provide relevant connections. Otto (2018) states that for young children, "the riddles and jokes they create are often based in semantic comparisons or words that have multiple meanings" (248).

Infusion of culturally relevant literacy tools that promote oracy must be planned. Table 6.4 shows how a lesson related to animals and their habitat can be infused with *adivinanzas* and *canciones*. In this case, we provide an example within a bilingual model that alternates oral language development by days: Monday (Spanish), Tuesday (English), Wednesday (Spanish), Thursday (English), and Friday (Spanish).

Table 6.4. Use of Riddles and Sayings in a Dual Language Classroom

Monday: Spanish	Tuesday: English	Wednesday: Spanish	Thursday: English	Friday: Spanish
Adivinanzas (Riddles)				
Tómame con cuidado, *pues a veces soy muy chiquitita,* *y cuando tú me siembras* *me transformo en plantita.*	I travel very slowly When gliding along the ground Maybe my shell weighs me down In your garden I am found.	*Tómame con cuidado,* *pues a veces soy muy chiquitita,* *y cuando tú me siembras* *me transformo en plantita.*	I travel very slowly When gliding along the ground Maybe my shell weighs me down In your garden I am found.	*Tómame con cuidado,* *pues a veces soy muy chiquitita,* *y cuando tú me siembras* *me transformo en plantita.*
Canciones (Songs)				
"La araña pequeñita" (José Luis Orozco)	"Itsy Bitsy Spider"	*"La araña pequeñita"* (José Luis Orozco)	"Itsy Bitsy Spider"	*"La araña pequeñita"* (José Luis Orozco)

Strategies such as word walls, partner-based interactions, and riddles contribute to establishing predictable routines. These routines, however, may be difficult to follow for children with disabilities. Brillante (2017) recommends being intentional, systematic, and patient as we draw on children's strengths. Focusing on what children with learning disabilities can do in the context of the learning sequence presented in this chapter means:

> Ensuring that Phase 1 includes opportunities to figure things out as materials are manipulated and explored.

> Using Phase 2 and 3 of the learning sequences to write and read stories that are above children's reading levels. Brillante (2017) reminds us that "most children with disabilities have a high level of understanding and sophisticated listening vocabulary" (124).

The songs and riddles can be part of the morning routines to help set the tone for the learning that will take place and will reinforce the big and relevant ideas discussed throughout the unit or lesson. They also provide closure and infuse a sense of enjoyment as children sign, move, or play with words within the riddle to review what they know.

Summary

In any early childhood setting, the language development of DLLs follows patterns that are very similar to monolingual English-speaking children—that is, they initially develop receptive language at rates that are significantly higher in comparison to their expressive skills. It is estimated that by age 3, children's receptive vocabulary is four times greater than their expressive vocabulary (Jalongo & Sobolak 2011). As young children participate in Phases 1, 2, and 3 of the proposed learning sequence, they engage in increasingly complex language tasks. An interdisciplinary approach to biliteracy development across the content areas involves purposeful efforts to build receptive and expressive vocabulary through developmentally, culturally, and linguistically appropriate practices.

To achieve growth in all domains, DLLs benefit from strategies that purposefully focus on language while learning content such as child-generated word walls and translingual partner activities. Canagarajah (2013) argues that biliteracy development is possible when teachers allow children to operate within contexts where "differences can be displayed freely and negotiated actively" (82). Educators know that in linguistically and culturally diverse contexts, children draw from an array of languages, dialects, and registers present in their linguistic repertoire to engage, construct meaning, and accomplish communicative tasks. In their role as facilitators, educators set the tone and establish rules that prioritize children's engagement rather than strictly adhering to a compartmentalized view of language.

Key Points to Remember!

> Young children easily engage in activities that involve active exploration and play; therefore, it is important because it reminds us that in order to develop literacy skills in two languages, educators should create responsive

and enticing contexts in which children can seamlessly engage in motivating and developmentally appropriate tasks that integrate all language skills while relating to concepts in all content areas (Konishi et al. 2014).

> When planning speaking and listening activities for DLLs, connections to previous knowledge are likely to promote active involvement while enhancing children's existing skills.

> Support for children's home language is essential because literacy skills that they acquire in their first language will transfer to their second language and vice versa, thus facilitating development of reading and writing skills in both languages (Goldenberg 2013).

> At the heart of a developmentally appropriate biliteracy approach is the idea that reading, writing, speaking, and listening are acquired in interconnected ways across the content areas (Beeman & Urow 2013).

> Young children benefit from experiences that integrate content and literacy and that advance from concrete to abstract (Kostelnik, Soderman, & Whiren 2011).

Frequently Asked Questions

How should educators respond to children's written or oral production as they mix languages or use a different language than expected?

One common misconception in the field of bilingual education leads educators to often overemphasize adherence to a specific language, generally the language of instruction. As educators plan and implement lessons that promote learning in two languages in the content areas, it is important to keep in mind the key distinction between language of instruction and language of learning, discussed in Chapter 3. Language of instruction must remain consistent and must be carefully planned and strategically used. Language of learning refers to children's oral production as they engage in meaning making. Children's oral production may or may not match language of instruction. That is not concerning, as long as children maintain focus on the concept and demonstrate understanding.

Should educators post a word wall in more than one language?

Two word walls, one for each language of instruction (e.g., English and Spanish, English and Vietnamese), are recommended because each will provide opportunities to compare languages and discuss similarities and differences. There is no need, however, to translate or provide all words in both languages.

References

Alanís, I. 2013. "Where's My Partner? Developing Effective Bilingual Pairs for Dual Language Classrooms." *Young Children* 68 (1): 42–47.

Arreguín-Anderson, M.G., & I. Alanís. 2019. *Translingual Partners in Early Childhood Elementary-Education: Pedagogies on Linguistic and Cognitive Engagement.* New York: Peter Lang Publishing.

Arreguín-Anderson, M.G., & J.A. Ruiz-Escalante. 2015. "Dichos and Adivinanzas: Literary

Resources that Enhance Science Learning and Teaching in the Bilingual Classroom." In *Multilingual Literature for Latino Bilingual Children: Their Words, Their Worlds,* eds. E. Riojas-Clark, B. Bustos-Flores, H.L. Smith, D.A. González, 167–82. Lanham, MD: Rowman & Littlefield.

Beeman, K., & C. Urow. 2013. *Teaching for Biliteracy: Strengthening Bridges Between Languages.* Philadelphia: Caslon Publishing.

Brillante, P. 2017. *The Essentials: Supporting Young Children with Disabilities in the Classroom.* Washington, DC: NAEYC.

Canagarajah, S. 2013. *Translingual Practice: Global Englishes and Cosmopolitan Relation.* New York: Routledge.

Contant, T.L., J. Bass, A. Tweed, & A.A. Carin. 2018. *Teaching Science Through Inquiry-Based Instruction.* New York: Pearson.

Escamilla, K., S. Hopewell, S. Butvilofsky, W. Sparrow, L. Soltero-González, O. Ruiz-Figueroa, & M. Escamilla. 2014. *Biliteracy from the Start: Litreacy Squared in Action.* Philadelphia: Caslon.

Goldenberg, C. 2013. "Unlocking the Research on English Learners: What We Know—and Don't Yet Know—About Effective Instruction." *American Educator* 37 (2): 4–11.

Hoffman, J., M. Collins, & J.A. Schickedanz. 2015. "Instructional Challenges in Developing Young Children's Science Concepts." *Reading Teacher* 68 (5): 363–72.

Jalongo, M., & M. Sobolak. 2011. "Supporting Young Children's Vocabulary Growth: The Challenges, the Benefits, and Evidence-Based Strategies." *Early Childhood Education Journal* 38 (6): 421–29.

Konishi, H., J. Kanero, M.R. Freeman, R. Michnick Golinkoff, & K. Hirsh-Pasek. 2014. "Six Principles of Language Development: Implications for Second Language Learners." *Developmental Neuropsychology* 39 (5): 404–20.

Kostelnik, M.J., A.K. Soderman, A.P. Whiren, & M.L. Rupiper. 2019. *Developmentally Appropriate Curriculum: Best Practices in Early Childhood Education.* 7th ed. Boston: Pearson.

NASEM (National Academies of Sciences, Engineering, and Medicine). 2017. *Promoting the Educational Success of Children and Youth Learning English: Promising Futures.* Washington, DC: National Academies Press. doi:10.17226/24677.

Otto, B. 2018. *Language Development in Early Childhood.* Upper Saddle River, NJ: Pearson.

Rivas, O. 2015. "Facilitación de actividades colaborativas de parejas bilingües en un aula de primaria: Analizando su efectividad en el aprendizaje estudiantil." Master's thesis. ProQuest (UMI No. 1592696).

Soltero-González, L., & I. Reyes. 2012. "Literacy Practices and Language Use Among Latino Emergent Bilingual Children in Preschool Contexts." In *Early Biliteracy Development: Exploring Young Learners' Use of Their Linguistic Resources,* eds. E.B. Bauer & M. Gort, 34–54. New York: Routledge.

Stein, P. 2008. *Multimodal Pedagogies in Diverse Classrooms: Representation, Rights, and Resources.* London: Routledge.

naeyc® Accreditation

Early Learning Programs

This chapter supports the following NAEYC Early Learning Program Accreditation Standards and Topic Areas:

Standard 3: Teaching

3.A Designing Enriched Learning Environments

3.D Using Time, Grouping, and Routines to Achieve Learning Goals

7 Learning Through a Second Language

Objectives

> Explain the significance of comprehensible input for dual language learners.

> Discuss the need for quality language interactions.

> Share culturally authentic practices that promote a bilingual identity.

> Discuss strategies that strengthen and support children's overall development.

The Almusaad family recently emigrated to the United States. Their 4-year-old daughter, Haifa, will be attending a state-funded prekindergarten program. She speaks Arabic at home and a little English. Her parents recently had a productive meeting with her teacher, Mrs. Siller, discussing Haifa's language experiences. As the family walks away, Mrs. Siller, who has a certification in English as a second language, is feeling uncertain about how she will best meet the needs of her DLLs because this year she has four other languages represented in her classroom.

This vignette represents the reality for many teachers and children in US schools. Research indicates bilingual education is the most effective approach for the long-term academic achievement of DLLs (Barnett et al. 2007; NASEM 2017; Thomas & Collier 2017). However, the lack of qualified bilingual teachers in the diverse languages represented in early childhood classrooms and the various educational policies result in many classrooms in which young DLLs do not have access to instruction in their home language. Teachers must, however, develop the English language and literacy skills of DLLs while supporting their home language. This may not be an easy task, but it is not impossible. Effective teachers use a range of instructional strategies to accommodate children's development and learning; are intentional in their design of lessons, activities, and assessments; and have an asset-driven belief about bilingualism to incorporate the native language of DLLs in the classroom (Baker & Páez 2018; Epstein 2014; Espinosa 2009). They are also reflective practitioners who seek out additional resources and professional development to assist them with their practice (Derman-Sparks & Ramsey 2011).

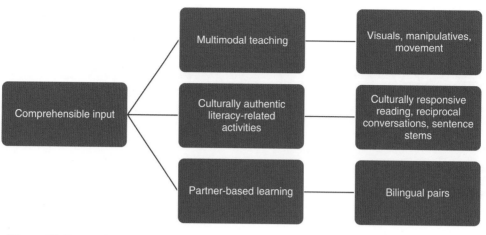

Figure 7.1. Comprehensible input.

In this chapter, we provide developmentally, culturally, and linguistically appropriate strategies that teachers can apply within multiple contexts but that are critical when working with DLLs. We use examples from two classrooms—Mrs. Siller's prekindergarten English as a second language (ESL) classroom and Mrs. Dion's dual language Spanish–English kindergarten classroom. Children in Mrs. Dion's class are learning through two languages. There are times in the day when Spanish-speaking children are learning content in English and other times when English-speaking children are learning in Spanish. We use these two classrooms to illustrate how all teachers can use the strategies to facilitate learning vocabulary and concepts through a second language. These strategies are also effective when teaching children with disabilities.

Using a socio-constructivist philosophy (Vygotsky 1978), we focus on strategies that build on children's cultural and linguistic experiences. Under this philosophy, children are viewed as active participants who learn by interacting with peers at varying developmental levels. Through social interactions, children use all modes of language: reading, writing, speaking, and listening. To ensure all children are successful, teachers should make sure that information is comprehensible. In other words, teachers use visuals or gestures to help children understand what is being communicated. In addition, teachers should infuse their lessons, activities, and routines with multimodal teaching, culturally authentic literacy related activities, and partner-based learning strategies (see Figure 7.1). Although we present each of these in separate sections, effective teachers will use multiple aspects of these strategies at the same time.

Comprehensible Input

When working with DLLs, the best methods are those that "supply 'comprehensible input' in low anxiety situations, containing messages that students really want to hear" (Krashen 1982, 6). In other words, teachers must ensure DLLs understand and can engage with the information presented. This means they cannot rely on language alone but must use additional strategies and materials to scaffold children's learning. Otherwise, DLLs will struggle to decipher what the teacher is saying and what he expects them to accomplish. As a result, DLLs miss grade-level instruction and fall behind their English-speaking peers. To develop instruction that advances children's thinking and develops their self-efficacy as learners, teachers need to integrate multimodal teaching strategies that utilize various modes of learning.

Strategies for Multimodal Teaching

Children develop their understanding of the world using all of their senses. Multimodal teaching strategies respond to children's individual ways of learning—auditory, visual, tactile, and kinesthetic. Tapping into how children learn helps them stay engaged and motivated; as a result, they understand and retain more information. For DLLs, the strategies help make the information comprehensible. Using various modes allows you to present information in more than one way, increase the participation of DLLs, and provide different opportunities for children to show you their capabilities and strengths. In this section, we focus on visual cues and representations, pictures, objects and manipulatives, and movement to assist DLLs with their learning and development.

Using Children's Senses

Multimodal teaching can include activities that tap into children's senses, like the following:

> Listening: songs related to your topic, listening cans, nature walk

> Visual: anchor charts, illustrations, I Spy games

> Smell: food extracts, scented and spice-filled jars

> Touch: sensory cards, sand and water play, flannel boards, surprise box

> Taste: taste tests with sweet, sour, salty foods

Visual Cues and Representations

To facilitate learning, effective teachers augment lessons and children's activities with visual cues and representations such as pictures and objects. Visuals also support children with disabilities as they provide aided communication strategies (Brillante 2017).

Pictures

Pictures help DLLs associate words or concepts with an image and connect with their previous experiences or knowledge. For example, when shown a picture of a parrot, many DLLs will know about birds (e.g., they have wings and fly) but might not have the label(s) in English. The picture allows them to capitalize on their wealth of knowledge in their home language and apply it to what they are learning in their second language. Mrs. Dion created picture cards to represent various community helpers and labeled each one with the corresponding title. Similarly, Mrs. Siller asked children's family members to contribute pictures of their jobs or professions.

In both classrooms, children used the pictures to discuss the various professions, draw what they wanted to be, and label the tools used by each community helper. Many curriculum programs provide sets of thematic pictures, but you can also search the internet for relevant images or take your own pictures of items found at home or around the school. You can also take pictures of children engaged in actions or behaviors you are reinforcing or teaching.

Objects and Manipulatives

Real-life objects, props, or artifacts provide a concrete representation of vocabulary words and concepts. Objects are more effective than pictures because children can see and hold them—appealing to visual and kinesthetic learners. Mrs. Dion, for example, created a large clock that children could manipulate when discussing the concept of time. Mrs. Siller frequently brought in objects to use during daily read-alouds.

Manipulatives are learning tools that provide concrete hands-on experiences for children to make meaning of abstract concepts. Similar to objects, manipulatives can be anything that children can touch and move. Manipulatives include Unifix cubes, interlocking cubes, tiles, and counters children can use to develop a variety of math concepts.

In Mrs. Dion's classroom, children explore repeating patterns with rocks, leaves, shells, interlocking cubes, and tiles. Children frequently switch manipulatives, such as creating a pattern with rocks and then showing that same pattern with interlocking cubes to their peers. Clara (a native English speaker) selects large and small shells to illustrate her AB pattern to Alex (a native Spanish speaker). After observing Clara complete a few examples, Alex searches for different-shaped

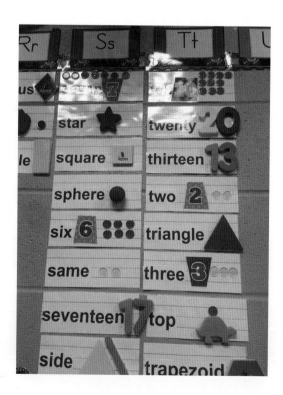

shells to create his own AB pattern. He then points to his pattern and asks Clara, in Spanish, to pick a shell that represents the next one in his pattern. As he asks her, he uses gestures to help Clara understand his request.

Mrs. Dion created a hands-on activity where DLLs could learn from their peers, exchange ideas, and apply their understanding by pointing to or moving the manipulatives.

Movement

It is a developmental expectation that young children need to move around. Movement is an effective kinesthetic strategy that gets children energized and engaged. Teachers can integrate movement through gestures, total physical response, music, and dance. These strategies also individualize support and can serve as curricular modifications for children with disabilities (Brillante 2017).

Children in Mrs. Siller's classroom used movement to learn about math concepts. They created movements and rhythmic clapping to represent patterns. In the following exchange, we see how Mrs. Siller engages Monica (a native Spanish speaker) and Stephanie (a native English speaker).

> **Mrs. Siller:** Do you think you could show this same pattern by using movement? Watch me—*pat, clap, snap, pat, clap, snap.*
>
> **Monica:** (*Hesitantly repeats the pat, clap, snap pattern.*)
>
> **Stephanie:** We could also do patterns with our legs and feet! This one is clap, stomp, stomp, clap, stomp, stomp—it's a clap and two stomps!
>
> **Mrs. Siller:** Did you see that, Monica? She did clap, stomp, stomp. Which pattern could that be? (*Points to the various pattern examples on the wall.*)
>
> **Monica:** (*Points to the pattern that matches an ABB pattern.*)
>
> **Mrs. Siller**: That's right, it follows an ABB pattern. Let's try another one.

Mrs. Siller used movement, visuals, and a peer to make her instruction comprehensible. Note that although Monica is still developing her expressive English skills, she has developed receptive language to understand Mrs. Siller's directions and the pattern concept.

Gestures

Gestures provide another means to communicate. Earlier we saw how Alex used gestures to communicate with Clara. Both Mrs. Siller and Mrs. Dion frequently used exaggerated gestures and body movement to communicate intent. For example, when it was time to line up, Mrs. Siller provided the oral directions but she also bent her knees to act out the motion of standing from a seated position. She added hand motions to signal for everyone to stand up. She walked over to the door and gestured for children to follow her. These physical movements provided a visual scaffold for DLLs to understand her English words.

Total physical response (TPR)
A specific ESL strategy designed to provide children with gestures that will help them learn vocabulary in a second language (Asher 1966).

mix-pair-share

A Kagan cooperative learning structure where children walk or dance around the classroom to partner with a peer. You can integrate music to signal when children should stop and find a partner to share their ideas, responses to a question, or description of an object. When the music restarts, the cycle begins again.

Total Physical Response

Total physical response (TPR) is a specific ESL strategy designed to provide children with gestures that will help them learn vocabulary in a second language (Asher 1966). Children listen to a command in a second language and immediately respond with the appropriate physical action. The physical movement creates a link between words and action. For example, Mrs. Dion frequently combined TPR with songs that included hand movements representing the characteristics of mountains (hands above their heads together to form a point) and oceans (hands flowing in front of them). The visual and kinesthetic connections to new vocabulary also make TPR an effective strategy to support children with disabilities.

Music and Dance

Using music and dance is an effective and fun strategy that almost all children enjoy. Mrs. Dion regularly used the cooperative learning strategy of **mix-pair-share** to get children dancing around the room as they looked for a partner to talk with. Music and dancing enhanced children's socioemotional and linguistic skills but also tapped into children's need for movement.

Strategies for Authentic Literacy-Related Instruction

The use of culturally and linguistically authentic instruction builds connections to children's home language and cultural wealth and encourages their social patterns of behavior (Gutiérrez & Rogoff 2003). Culturally responsive teachers recognize that children express their cultural knowledge in the language they use, the manner in which they play, the stories they tell, and in interactions with others (Brown-Jeffy & Cooper 2011). Effective educators use this knowledge to create language-rich experiences where children can listen to and use language in meaningful activities as they develop their bilingual identities and early literacy skills (Castro et al. 2011). Recent research finds that "young children can attain proficiency in more than one language provided they have sufficient language input" (NASEM 2017, 23). The quality of teacher input has led to higher language scores and increased vocabulary growth for DLLs (Aukrust 2007; Bowers & Va Silyeva 2011). Language input is necessary for language acquisition, but so is language output (Ribot, Hoff, & Burridge 2018). Literacy-related activities and reciprocal conversations lead to an increase in the listening, speaking, reading, and writing skills of DLLs (Gillanders, Castro, & Franco 2014).

Culturally Relevant Stories

Read-alouds, shared reading, and storytelling lead to increased listening skills, vocabulary, and engagement with written text (Cummins 2011; Massaro 2015). Effective early childhood teachers integrate culturally relevant picture books and oral stories that support children's connections to their cultural knowledge, linguistic identity, and previous experiences (Purcell-Gates et al. 2011). Consider the following two examples of readings that connect to children's backgrounds:

When learning about family customs and traditions, Mrs. Dion reads Alma Flor Ada's *I Love Saturdays y domingos*. In this bilingual text, children learn about a young girl who enjoys spending Saturdays with her Euro-American, English-speaking grandparents and spending *los domingos* (Sundays) with her Mexican, Spanish-speaking grandparents. This reflects the family setting of many children who live between two cultural and linguistic worlds.

Mrs. Siller reads the bilingual book *René Has Two Last Names*, by René Colato Laínez, which is about the use of two last names in the Latino culture. The first is the father's surname and the second is the mother's maiden name. She uses the reading to develop children's early literacy skills and their cultural identity.

Both teachers used a **dialogic reading** strategy to promote language interactions and various emergent literacy skills. Before the reading, the teachers identified vocabulary to focus on and asked the children to repeat the words as they were read. They also developed open-ended questions to help the children make connections with their cultural knowledge and previous experiences. This strategy can also create space for turn-and-talk opportunities, during which children develop their competence and confidence with language (Bolt et al. 2019). In Mrs. Dion's and Mrs. Siller's classrooms, the children used their home language, English, or a combination of both to communicate and develop positive relationships with others. This flexibility and freedom with language increased the amount and complexity of children's language.

dialogic reading

A reading practice using picture books where adults ask simple questions and then follow up with expanded questions (Whitehurst et al. 1988). Research indicates this interactive discussion between an adult and child(ren) improves literacy and language skills because adults intentionally focus on vocabulary, story elements, and narrative skills (Brannon & Dauksas 2014; Lever & Sénéchal 2011).

Finding and Using Culturally Appropriate Texts

> Seek out families as resources for book selections.

> Reach out to your local library.

> Examine culturally relevant texts for cultural accuracy, realistic lifestyles, believable characters, and authentic language.

> Have children create their own storybooks.

> Invite families or members of the community to read a familiar picture book in their native language or share a family story.

Reciprocal Conversations

DLLs benefit from reciprocal conversations with adults and peers that augment their oral language and socioemotional skills as they enhance cognitive development (Castro et al. 2011; Hoff 2006). These oral language skills provide the foundation for literacy. During reciprocal conversations, adults can model the back-and-forth nature of conversations by asking questions that require children to use their language skills. Teachers can expand on children's language through verbal mapping and repeating what they say. When engaging in these conversations, consider your responses to children. Quality interactions involve a balance between teacher- and child-directed conversations, active listening, smiling, and making eye contact. Keep in mind, DLLs may need time to process what you say in English because they often translate the message into their home language before responding. Provide children with the time they need. These behaviors send a message that the child has value, has something important to say, and has agency.

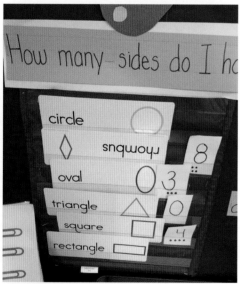

Sentence Stems

Developmentally appropriate and linguistically accessible sentence stems (a scaffold to help students respond in complete sentences) help children engage in reciprocal conversations with others and promote the use of academic language. DLLs often know what they want to say in their home language but are unsure of how to say it in their second language. Sentence stems scaffold sentence structure and augment language usage. For example, Mrs. Dion noticed that children were using one-word responses in conversations with their partners (e.g., "doctor"). She encouraged children to use the sentence "I want to be a _____" instead. Children quickly adopted the English syntax as they told their peers what they wanted to be when they grew up. During her math lesson, Mrs. Siller created written sentence stems related to shapes. Children used the sentence "I am a _____" and a picture card when they were playing a guessing game to determine the shape of an object. The sentence stem and the picture cards provided children with the math vocabulary and the name of the shape in English as they engaged in math conversations with a peer.

Partner-Based Learning Strategy

Vygotsky (1978) asserted that learning occurs when children interact with others in intentional and meaningful ways. These interactions among children are significant for oral language development because they promote communication and language production (Ramírez-Esparza, García-Sierra, & Kuhl 2016). This active view of learning coincides with developmentally appropriate practice, which suggests developing multiple domains through active pedagogical approaches (Copple & Bredekamp 2009). Intentional teachers invite children to talk with each other through meaningful activities (Arreguín-Anderson & Alanís 2019; Epstein 2014). One strategy all teachers can use is partner-based learning (Alanís 2013). This strategy provides opportunities for all children to process and verbalize what they are learning, enhances their social skills, promotes active engagement, and reduces anxiety (Johnson & Johnson 1994).

zone of proximal development (ZPD)
A concept developed by Lev Vygotsky (1978) that explains the range of ability between what children can do alone versus what they can do with assistance from a more knowledgeable other. Social interaction is a critical part of this process. For example, buddy reading allows stronger readers to assist peers with the reading process by modeling reading strategies, asking questions, or explaining the process.

Effective teachers facilitate peer conversations through hands-on, interactive activities that are connected to children's previous experiences (Copple et al. 2013). Mrs. Siller and Mrs. Dion partnered children heterogeneously by language and content ability to create a space for intellectual and linguistic growth or **zone of proximal development (ZPD).** Children engaged with their partners during learning center time, whole group discussions, and hands-on activities as illustrated here:

> Mrs. Siller provides various manipulatives for pairs of children to sort. Bekisizwe and Ani begin to sort the shared items. As they sort, Bekisizwe taps Ani on the arm and excitedly shows her his categories of size and shape. Initially Ani is only sorting items by color. Then she observes the ways in which Bekisizwe is categorizing the objects and begins to replicate what he is doing. Eventually their sorting categories grow to include size, shape, color, and texture.

Mrs. Siller enhanced children's level of understanding through a hands-on activity where they could try out different sorting categories by observing and actively engaging with a peer. When children are engaged in partner-based learning, they will play, solve problems, negotiate meanings, and share ideas with peers (Epstein 2014).

When using a partner-based learning strategy, consider the following:

> Use heterogeneous partnerships based on children's language levels, their personalities, and their understanding of concepts (Arreguín-Anderson & Alanís 2019).

> Provide explicit modeling of the shared process of learning (Alanís & Arreguín-Anderson 2019).

> Establish guidelines for turn taking (e.g., eye contact, physically turning to face each other) and practice these throughout the school day (Bolt et al. 2019).

> Have pairs share materials to encourage the shared construction of knowledge through listening and thinking (Bedrova & Leong 2015).

> Provide visual or auditory cues so that children know when to take turns, such as using different colored pencils, shaking a tambourine, or setting a timer on your phone.

> Designate A/B roles with tangible objects (e.g., shapes, rubber bracelets). Assign a task for each role.

> Pair children with more socially knowledgeable peers (Park & Lee 2015) and have them remain with the same partner for an extended amount of time.

These collaborative learning opportunities promote active participation, increase language input and output, and send the implicit message that all children have something important to contribute.

Summary

The daily experiences children have in classrooms influence their approach to learning and the way they feel about themselves as learners. Teachers who create opportunities for children to interact, talk, move, and learn from each other create quality language environments that promote the learning and development of DLLs. Interactive and hands-on activities promote active participation where children can tap into their previous cultural and linguistic experiences. Comprehensible input through linguistic and strategic supports allows children to take risks with language and encourage children's agency as active participants in their learning. All of this enhances their schooling experience as children augment their cultural and linguistic assets to construct their bilingual identities.

Key Points to Remember!

> Tapping into how children learn helps them stay engaged and motivated; as a result, they understand and retain more information.

> Movement is an effective kinesthetic strategy that gets children energized and engaged. Teachers can integrate movement through gestures, total physical response, music, and dance.

> "Young children can attain proficiency in more than one language provided they have sufficient language input" (NASEM 2017, 23).

> Quality interactions involve a balance between teacher- and child-directed conversations, active listening, smiling, and making eye contact.

> Sentence stems scaffold sentence structure and augment language usage.

> Intentional teachers invite children to talk with each other through meaningful activities (Arreguín-Anderson & Alanís 2019; Epstein 2014).

> When children are engaged in partner-based learning, they will play, solve problems, negotiate meanings, and share ideas with peers (Epstein 2014).

Frequently Asked Questions

Should I make my lessons easier so that DLLs will understand?

We do not want to reduce the level of rigor for children. When teachers lower their expectations, they also lower the rate of progress DLLs make. This means they will not develop at the same rate as their English-speaking peers and will fall further and further behind. Instead, scaffold their learning with contextual and linguistic supports to make the information comprehensible. The use of visuals, gestures, sentence stems, and peers will help children access and understand the information presented. Understand that learning in a second language is a developmental process that takes time.

Can I use these second language learning strategies with my non-DLLs?

Yes, these strategies are effective practices for all children. For example, visuals help all children learn new vocabulary and content. Partner-based hands-on activities allow children to show you what they know and what they are capable of. These strategies lead to active learning, interactions with peers at varying developmental levels, and the integration of language modes of reading, writing, speaking, and listening.

References

Alanís, I. 2013. "Where's My Partner? Developing Effective Bilingual Pairs for Dual Language Classrooms." *Young Children* 68 (1): 42–47.

Alanís, I., & M.G. Arreguín-Anderson. 2019. "Paired Learning: Strategies for Enhancing Social Competence in Dual Language Classrooms." *Young Children* 74 (2): 6–12.

Arreguín-Anderson, M.G., & I. Alanís. 2019. *Translingual Partners in Early Childhood Elementary-Education: Pedagogies on Linguistic and Cognitive Engagement.* New York: Peter Lang Publishing.

Asher, J.R. 1966. "The Total Physical Response Technique of Learning." *Journal of Special Education* 3 (3): 253–62.

Aukrust, V.G. 2007. "Young Children Acquiring Second Language Vocabulary in Preschool Group-Time: Does Amount, Diversity, and Discourse Complexity of Teacher Talk Matter?" *Journal of Research in Childhood Education* 22 (1): 17–37.

Baker, M., & M. Páez. 2018. *The Language of the Classroom: Dual Language Learners in Head Start, Public PreK, and Private Preschool Programs.* Washington, DC: Migration Policy Institute.

Barnett, W.S., J.T. Hustedt, A.H. Friedman, J.S. Boyd, & P. Ainsworth. 2007. *The State of Preschool 2007.* Report. New Brunswick, NJ: National Institute for Early Education Research. http://nieer.org/wp-content/uploads/2016/10/2007yearbook.pdf.

Bedrova, E., & D.J. Leong. 2015. "Vygotskian and Post-Vygotskian Views on Children's Play." *American Journal of Play* 7 (3): 371–87.

Bolt, M.E., C.M. Rodriguez, C.J. Wagner, & C.P. Proctor. 2019. "Can We Talk? Creating Opportunities for Meaningful Academic Discussions with Multilingual Children." *Young Children* 74 (2): 40–47.

Bowers, E.P., & M. Va Silyeva. 2011. "The Relation Between Teacher Input and Lexical Growth of Preschoolers." *Applied Psycholinguistics* 32 (1): 221–41.

Brannon, D., & L. Dauksas. 2014. "The Effectiveness of Dialogic Reading in Increasing English Language Learning Preschool Children's Expressive Language." *International Research in Early Childhood Education* 5 (1): 1–10.

Brillante, P. 2017. *The Essentials: Supporting Young Children with Disabilities in the Classroom.* Washington, DC: NAEYC.

Brown-Jeffy, S., & J.E. Cooper. 2011. "Toward a Conceptual Framework of Culturally Relevant Pedagogy: An Overview of the Conceptual and Theoretical Literature." *Teacher Education Quarterly* 38 (1): 65–84.

Castro, D.C., M. Páez, D. Dickinson, & E. Frede. 2011. "Promoting Language and Literacy in Dual Language Learners: Research, Practice, and Policy." *Child Development Perspectives* 5 (1): 15–21.

Copple, C., & S. Bredekamp, eds. 2009. *Developmentally Appropriate Practice in Early Childhood Programs from Birth Through Age 8.* 3rd ed. Washington, DC: NAEYC.

Copple, C., S. Bredekamp, D. Koralek, & K. Charner, eds. 2013. *Developmentally Appropriate Practice: Focus on Preschoolers.* Washington, DC: NAEYC.

Cummins, J. 2011. "Literacy Engagement: Fueling Academic Growth for English Learners." *Reading Teacher* 65 (2): 142–46.

Derman-Sparks, L., & P.G. Ramsey. 2011. *What If All the Kids Are White? Anti-Bias Multicultural Education with Young Children and Families.* 2nd ed. New York: Teachers College Press.

Epstein, A.S. 2014. *The Intentional Teacher: Choosing the Best Strategies for Young Children's Learning.* Rev. ed. Washington, DC: NAEYC; Ypsilanti, MI: HighScope.

Espinosa, L.M. 2009. *Getting It Right for Young Children from Diverse Backgrounds: Applying Research to Improve Practice.* Boston: Pearson.

Gillanders, C., D.C. Castro, & X. Franco. 2014. "Learning Words for Life: Promoting Vocabulary in Dual Language Learners." *Reading Teacher* 68 (3): 213–21.

Gutiérrez, K.D., & B. Rogoff. 2003. "Cultural Ways of Learning: Individual Traits or Repertoires of Practice." *Educational Researcher* 32 (5): 19–25.

Hoff, E. 2006. "How Social Contexts Support and Shape Language Development." *Developmental Review* 26 (1): 55–88.

Johnson, D.W., & R.T. Johnson. 1994. *Learning Together and Alone: Cooperative, Competitive and Individualistic Learning.* 4th ed. Boston: Allen & Bacon.

Krashen, S.D. 1982. *Principles and Practices in Second Language Acquisition.* Oxford: Pergamon Press.

Lever, R., & M. Sénéchal. 2011. "Discussing Stories: On How Dialogic Reading Intervention Improves Kindergarteners' Oral Narrative Construction." *Journal of Experimental Child Psychology* 108 (1): 1–24.

Massaro, D. 2015. "Two Different Communication Genres and Implications for Vocabulary Development and Learning to Read." *Journal of Literacy Research* 47 (4): 505–27.

NASEM (National Academies of Sciences, Engineering, and Medicine). 2017. *Promoting the Educational Success of Children and Youth Learning English: Promising Futures.* Washington, DC: National Academies Press. doi:10.17226/24677.

Park, J., & J. Lee. 2015. "Dyadic Collaboration Among Preschool-Age Children and the Benefits of Working with a More Socially Advanced Peer." *Early Education and Development* 26 (4): 574–93.

Purcell-Gates, V., G. Melzi, N. Behnosh, & M.F. Orellana. 2011. "Building Literacy Instruction from Children's Sociocultural Worlds." *Child Development Perspectives* 5 (1): 22–27.

Ramírez-Esparza, N., A. García-Sierra, & P.K. Kuhl. 2016. "The Impact of Early Social Interactions on Later Language Development in Spanish–English Bilingual Infants." *Child Development* 88 (4):1216–34.

Ribot, K.M., E. Hoff, & A. Burridge. 2018. "Language Use Contributes to Expressive Language Growth: Evidence from Bilingual Children." *Child Development* 89 (3): 929–40.

Thomas, W., & V. Collier. 2017. "Validating the Power of Bilingual Schooling: Thirty-Two Years of Large-Scale, Longitudinal Research." *Annual Review of Applied Linguistics* 37: 203–17.

Whitehurst, G.J., F.L. Falco, C.J. Lonigan, J.E. Fischel, B.D. DeBaryshe, M.C. Valdez-Menchaca, & M. Caulfield. 1988. "Accelerating Language Development Through Picture Book Reading." *Development Psychology* 24 (4): 552–59. doi:10.1037/0012-1649.24.4.552.

Vygotsky, L.S. 1978. *Mind in Society: The Development of Higher Psychological Processes.* Cambridge: Harvard University Press.

naeyc™ **Accreditation**
Early Learning Programs

This chapter supports the following NAEYC Early Learning Program Accreditation Standards and Topic Areas:

Standard 3: Teaching

3.A Designing Enriched Learning Environments

3.B Creating Caring Communities for Learning

3.E Responding to Children's Interests and Needs

3.F Making Learning Meaningful for All Children

3.G Using Instruction to Deepen Children's Understanding and Build Their Skills and Knowledge

8 Designing Authentic Assessment

Objectives

> Recognize the need to develop reciprocal relationships with children's families throughout the assessment process.

> Describe the aspects of bilingualism that contribute to children's learning and development.

> Discuss the need for authentic assessments to capture emergent bilingual children's strengths and needs.

Four-year-old Francisco and his family recently emigrated from Guatemala. He is enrolled in a public Spanish–English dual language prekindergarten program. In conversations with his parents, Mrs. Sánchez learns that Francisco and his family speak an indigenous language and Spanish. Francisco's mother indicates Francisco is fluent in his indigenous language and has some Spanish fluency. As Mrs. Sánchez plans for instruction, she considers how she will determine if Francisco is making short-term and long-term progress in his language skills. She realizes she is unable to determine his proficiency in his home language but will need to assess his Spanish and emergent English skills.

Effective early childhood teachers, such as Mrs. Sánchez, use assessment to determine children's progress toward appropriate learning goals (Copple & Bredekamp 2009). These goals include children's linguistic strengths, cognition, and socioemotional development. In this chapter, we discuss assessment considerations when working with dual language learners. We emphasize the need to understand and assess the unique characteristics of DLLs from a strengths-based perspective and present strategies for authentic assessment. We concentrate on data-collection artifacts, including anecdotal notes, observations, photos, and audio and video recordings. These forms of assessment capture what children can do within a natural learning context.

The Purpose of Assessment

Assessment provides the opportunity to highlight and support children's learning process, their meaning-making strategies, and their interactions with peers (Arreguín-Anderson, Salinas-González, & Alanís 2018; García, Ibarra Johnson, & Seltzer 2017; Shabazian 2016).

To examine the growth and development of DLLs through developmentally, culturally, and linguistically appropriate assessment practices, teachers must

> Partner with children's families to determine children's strengths based on cultural, linguistic, and social contexts (Espinosa 2005; Michael-Luna 2013)

> Know children's capabilities appropriate to their age, developmental status, and linguistic skills within multiple contexts (Caspe et al. 2018; Moreno & Klute 2011).

> Identify appropriate assessment measures that are responsive to children's learning progress and in a combination of languages (García, Ibarra Johnson, & Seltzer 2017; García & Kleyn 2016).

> Use continuous assessment with varied types of information to inform instruction (Elicker & Benson McMullan 2013).

Engaging Families as Partners in the Assessment Process

All children develop within a sociocultural context immersed in their home and community (Vygotsky 1978). Therefore, children's families are a reliable source of information about their children and their learning environment (Michael-Luna 2013). Reciprocal relationships with families help teachers develop a collaborative approach to assessment where both parties understand the others' viewpoints and expectations (Copple & Bredekamp 2009). Mrs. Sánchez understands how these collaborations provide her with valuable information about children's behavior, learning preferences, and language skills. Through her conversations with Francisco's family, she develops a more complete view of his early learning and experiences at home, which helps her build on his capabilities and existing knowledge.

Establishing Reciprocal Conversations: Ascertaining Linguistic Strengths

Reciprocal conversations allow teachers and families a space to discuss the integrated nature of the academic, linguistic, and sociocultural development of DLLs. To ascertain children's linguistic strengths, you will need to learn more about the language(s) they speak and hear at home. Home language surveys and conversations with families can help you ascertain this information. The **home language survey** is the most commonly used tool to help educators learn (1) what language(s) are spoken at home and (2) what language(s) children use most often and with whom. However, conversations with families provide a richer description of children's experiences with language. In Table 8.1, we identify several questions you might ask families.

home language survey
A questionnaire that helps educators identify what language(s) children speak/use most often and with whom and who will require assessment of their English language proficiency. This is to determine whether children are eligible for bilingual education.

Table 8.1. Questions for Families

What Members of Your Family Live in Your Home?	What Language(s) Does Your Family Speak Most Often?
What language does your child speak most often at home? With whom?	What language does your child hear most often at home? From whom?
What does your child do when he or she gets home from school?	In what other contexts does your child hear or use language (e.g., church, playground)?
In what language(s) does your child watch TV or movies? What are some of his or her favorite shows?	Who does your child play with most often? What language(s) does your child speak when he or she plays with family members or friends?
What does your family do for fun?	Are there any pets in your home?
What would you like to tell me about your child or family?	Do you have any hobbies or interests that you would like to share with your child's class?

Source: Adapted from Espinosa 2005.

These open-ended questions provide opportunities for a family to share multiple aspects of their child's home life and previous experiences that can assist you with instructional planning and your initial assessment of the child. Asking about other family members at home, for example, tells you if the child has older siblings or grandparents who speak in different languages. (For resources that can assist you in these conversations, see the "Additional Resources" section.)

Sharing Developmental Progress with the Families of DLLs

Teachers should share information about a child's progress on a daily basis as well as through planned family–teacher conferences. When planning for conferences, the first thing to include should be an invitation to meet. Keep in mind, immigrant families may come from countries where family–teacher conferences are not the expectation. An invitation reassures families that they are welcome and encouraged to visit with their child's teacher. As mentioned in Chapter 1, it may be necessary for you to have an interpreter present and photographs or samples of a child's work to provide concrete examples of what the child is learning (Roller, Cunningham, Marin 2019). Ultimately, families should understand their children's progress is important to you and working together will help children meet established goals.

Helping Families Understand Goals and Expectations

> Develop templates of written communication in children's home language and English, addressing many of these topics, as well as milestones achieved and general progress.

the Ages & Stages Questionnaires (ASQ) and formal assessment systems such as the Receptive One-Word Picture Vocabulary Test; MyTeachingStrategies, GOLD; and the HighScope's Child Observation Record (COR) have versions in Spanish that can be used with Spanish-speaking DLLs.

It is also imperative to recognize that you have preferences and biases that will affect your judgment. Be self-aware and reflect on these biases to promote developmentally, culturally, and linguistically appropriate learning environments for DLLs. The use of multiple authentic assessment measures ensures the process meets these criteria.

Strategies for Authentic Assessment Measures

With authentic assessment, teachers document how children use skills and apply knowledge while engaging with materials and others in a natural setting (Mindes & Jung 2015). Gathering data within meaningful everyday activities allows you to capture the strengths and learning progression of DLLs across and within developmental domains (Blessing 2019; Seitz 2008). Although not an exhaustive list, in this section, we concentrate on systematic assessment through anecdotal notes, observations, photographs, and audio or video recordings as examples of meaningful assessment procedures for teachers and learners.

Facilitating Anecdotal Note-Taking

> Use sticky notes to capture how children are using their various language skills to communicate with their peers.

> Write quick notes and the date on the backs of writing samples to document what children are thinking as they write.

> Take photos or make a copy of what children are working on to attach to your notes (Bates, Schenck, & Hoover 2019).

Anecdotal Notes

Anecdotal notes can be short phrases or words that preserve important details, such as when children are using their Spanish phonetic skills to write in English or when they explain a concept using newly acquired academic language. When writing anecdotal notes, use strengths-based language that focuses on what children can do versus what they cannot do. For example, Mrs. Sánchez listened in as Francisco and Joaquin wrote sentences together. She noted that Francisco used the Spanish words *paloma* (dove), *ave* (bird), and *trampolín* (trampoline). From this, she determined his semantic strengths in Spanish and decided to provide pictures with English labels to augment Francisco's English learning.

Observations

Intentional observations help you gather data related to children's strengths and reflect on what the data indicates about children's progress (Mindes & Jung 2015). Carefully watching and listening to children helps you determine how they use language skills in different settings to communicate with other children, how their social skills are developing, and how they proceed from one stage to another in their play development. Observing children during their play and listening to them when they engage with other children is an effective means of determining their social and academic languages because children are less inhibited when talking with their peers (see Chapter 5). Observe children during daily moments of informal learning such as lunch and snack times, outdoor play, sociodramatic play, and child-directed learning.

Table 8.2. Sample Observation Form

Observation Form	Name of Child and Other Children Present	Date and Context
Objective for Observation (linguistic or content-based)		
What did you see?		
What did you hear?		
What communication strengths did you notice?		
What linguistic strengths did you notice?		
What content skills have children mastered?		
What are your next steps?		

Determine Purposeful Assessment

For observational assessment to be effective, you need to determine the purpose and the area of development of your assessment. It is necessary to distinguish the assessment of language proficiency with how DLLs use their languages to gain and reveal knowledge. For example, are you assessing to monitor children's language development or development of science concepts? Are you determining children's ability to communicate through writing or how effective they are with English grammar conventions? Understanding the purpose of the assessment will help you determine what assessment measure will provide valid and reliable information. For example, if you want to determine how a child is using language skills to communicate with peers, a video that captures verbal and nonverbal language might be more appropriate. Have specific questions in mind that focus on certain behaviors, individual children, or developmental skills. Then decide how to collect the information you are observing (e.g., checklist). Table 8.2 provides a sample observation form to help you establish a purpose for your observation. As you observe the child, ask yourself the following questions:

> How does the child communicate with others? (e.g., uses gestures, facial expressions, additional resources)

> What features of languaging is the child using? (e.g., substitutes another meaningful word to explain, asks questions related to objects, uses adjectives to describe, complexity of responses, language choice)

> How does the child reveal mastery of the objective(s)? (e.g., shows multiple ways to categorize, uses academic vocabulary, draws various patterns)

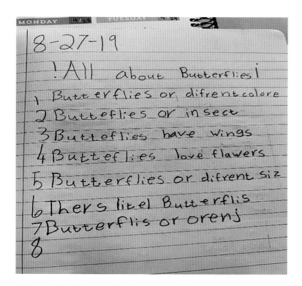

MONDAY 8/15

8-27-19

!All about Butterflies!
1 Butterflies or difrent colore
2 Butteflies or insect
3 Butteflies have wings
4 Butteflies love flawers
5 Butterflies or difrent siz
6 Thers litel Butterflis
7 Butterflis or orenj
8

Figure 8.1. Photo of Briana's writing exercise.

Photographic Documentation

Photographs provide evidence of learning at various stages and children's accomplishments. This is especially helpful with young DLLs who may not be able to articulate their learning. In Figure 8.1, we can see that Briana has mastered the following literacy skills:

> Use of title

> Spanish grammar skills for exclamation marks

> Invented spelling (e.g., *difrent, flawers, litel, orenj*)

> Strong use of conventional spelling (e.g., *about, insect, wings, love*)

> Ability to stay on topic

> Approximations such as using *or* for *are*

In addition to assessing how Briana uses language, it is important to go beyond language. What does she already know about written language and its purpose? When teachers observe the writing of DLLs and elicit their thinking, they have access to children's views of how different languages work (Gillanders & Soltero-Gonzalez 2019). By focusing on Briana's strengths, teachers can assess her individual development with the writing process and the ways she approaches the writing task.

Getting the Most from Photographic Documentation

> Take photos of children as they are completing a project to document how they approach a task.

> Use photos to show children's families the behaviors and skills their children are mastering within the classroom. These photos can be shared during in-person meetings or via email (Kroeger & Cardy 2006).

> Have children take photographs of their products, such as a block tower in the block center or their sorting of objects into buckets.

> Invite children to revisit photos, discuss them with peers, and reflect on their learning (Shabazian 2016).

Audio and Video Recordings

Audio and video recordings capture children's use of language and performance of a task. They give you the flexibility to hear or see things more than once. They also let you analyze children's speech within the actual context, allowing you to capture the setting and the other participants (Christie et al. 2014). Mrs. Sánchez video recorded children within their sociodramatic play center. This allowed her to see how children were using the objects and tools she had provided and hear the language(s) they were using. The videos showed that children needed novel props to keep them engaged in their play scenarios. From the videos, she also discovered that some children who were typically very quiet during other parts of the day were very active and vocal during their play time because they were free to use their language skills in a safe space.

When using audio or video recordings, consider the following:

> Choose times when children engage in relevant activities, with materials, and with others, such as during morning routines, whole group meetings, learning centers, and mealtimes.

> Focus on how children use social language and social skills to help each other with the meaning-making process (Arreguín-Anderson & Alanís 2019).

> Record children when they are telling their own stories. As you listen or watch, you will learn about their language and narrative skills, use of imagery or imagination, and cultural funds of knowledge (Gardner-Neblett & Iruka 2015).

> Record children during sociodramatic play to document how they are engaging in complex behavior that involves planning, self-monitoring, regulation of other's behavior, and reflection.

> Pay attention to their choice of language, purpose or function of the language, and the vocabulary used.

DLLs with Disabilities

DLLs may have a delay in language or speech development or other disabilities. For DLLs between the ages of 3 and 5, it may be difficult to distinguish between a language delay or disability and the natural stages of second language acquisition. Authentic assessment and survey tools that are available in other languages, such as the Ages & Stages Questionnaires (ASQ), can also help you identify young children who have developmental delays or disabilities. Keep in mind that it may be necessary to facilitate the family's completion of questionnaires to support their understanding of the items (Durán, forthcoming). Additionally, you need to include families and explain the process to them in terms they understand.

Often, educators refer DLLs for special education services because they are unsure of how to distinguish language and cognitive development (Rueda & Stillman 2012). Other times, educators hesitate to refer children for services for fear that their lack of progress is related to their bilingualism. It is crucial to seek support as early as possible. If you are unsure about a child's progress, reach out to

> Community members who understand the child's culture or language

> General education colleagues who can share strategies or curricular modifications that are most effective for young DLLs

> Bilingual education teachers who can help you distinguish between typical second language acquisition behaviors and language delays

Bilingual intervention for DLLs with a disability leads to greater growth in both languages (Guiberson & Ferris 2019). Whether in a bilingual or ESL classroom, educators must provide multitiered systems of support for young DLLs. When working with young DLLs, it is important to ensure a developmental delay is not actually an issue of comprehension and ineffective instruction. If DLLs are not receiving high-quality instruction, they will not make adequate progress. If the teacher is using the instructional strategies mentioned in Chapter 7 to make the content comprehensible, but the child is still not progressing, it may be a learning disability.

When assessing a DLL who you suspect has a delay or disability

> Use a variety of methods to gather information from multiple sources, including the child's family and other significant individuals in the child's life.

> Obtain information about the child's skills in daily activities, routines, and environments, such as at home, at your center, and in the community.

> Collaborate with other professionals and seek out additional information about bilingual development.

> Hire bilingual teaching assistants to support intervention services.

> Recognize that families will need support with the development of individualized service plans.

Summary

The assessment of DLLs is a complex process that requires careful consideration and planning. It is important to understand the range of language development found in DLLs and how it influences assessment outcomes. This knowledge leads to a more holistic picture of children's development. Using assessment in multiple languages and across learning domains will lead to authentic assessments that capture the capabilities of DLLs. This knowledge leads to a richer understanding of each child's learning and development, an enhanced collaboration between teachers and families, and a stronger sense of belonging and success for all children.

Key Points to Remember!

> Open-ended questions provide an opportunity for a family to share multiple aspects of a child's home life and previous experiences that can assist you with instructional planning and your initial assessment of the child.

> All children are born with the capacity to learn multiple languages.

> The National Academies of Sciences, Engineering, & Medicine recommends "developmental screening, observation, and ongoing assessment in both languages" to support planning for preschoolers using tools written in that language (NASEM 2017, 423).

> Gathering data within meaningful everyday activities allows you to capture the strengths and learning progression of DLLs across and within developmental domains (Blessing 2019; Seitz 2008).

> It is necessary to distinguish the assessment of language proficiency with how DLLs use their languages to gain and reveal knowledge.

> When teachers observe the writing of DLLs and elicit their thinking, they have access to children's views of how different languages work (Gillanders & Soltero-Gonzalez 2019).

> If DLLs are not receiving high-quality instruction, they will not make adequate progress.

Frequently Asked Questions

How can I assess what children know if I do not rely on language?

Use hands-on types of assessment, children's drawings, or photographs. For example, asking children to draw the various stages of the life cycle of a plant or animal allows them to demonstrate knowledge of that content. This way you can confirm their knowledge of science, not their English skills.

What if we do not have access to a screener in the child's home language?

It is best to have qualified bilingual staff assess a child's linguistic skills in the home language and in English. It might be helpful to bring in an interpreter, but keep in mind it is important that the interpreter understand the purpose of the assessment. If appropriate linguistic assessment tools are not available, you should interpret the results from an English test with consideration of these limitations.

What can I do if my school is inappropriately assessing bilingual children?

Identify the limitations of the standardized assessment outcomes. Advocate for the use of multiple measures, including information from families, for instructional purposes and program placement. Use authentic assessment to collect information about what the child can do in both languages.

In what language should DLLs receive support services?

Children should receive intervention or special services in their home language (NASEM 2017). Families need to communicate with children in their home language so that they build a strong foundation for their second language (Paradis 2010). Additionally, families need to use the recommended interventions with their child at home in their home language.

References

Arreguín-Anderson, M.G., & I. Alanís. 2019. *Translingual Partners in Early Childhood Elementary-Education: Pedagogies on Linguistic and Cognitive Engagement.* New York: Peter Lang Publishing.

Arreguín-Anderson, M., I. Salinas-González, & I. Alanís. 2018. "Translingual Play that Promotes Cultural Connections, Invention, and Regulation: A LatCrit Perspective." *International Multilingual Research Journal* 12 (4): 273–87.

Barrueco, S. 2012. *Assessing Spanish-English Bilingual Preschoolers: A Guide to Best Approaches and Measures.* Baltimore: Brookes.

Bates, C.C., S.M. Schenck, & H.J. Hoover. 2019. "Anecdotal Records: Practical Strategies for Taking Meaningful Notes." *Young Children* 74 (3): 14–19.

Blessing, A.D. 2019. "Assessment in Kindergarten: Meeting Children Where They Are." *Young Children* 74 (3): 6–13.

Caspe, M., A. Seltzer, J. Lorenzo Kennedy, M. Cappio, & C. Delorenzo. 2018. "Engaging Families in the Child Assessment Process." In *Spotlight on Young Children: Observation and Assessment,* eds. H. Bohart & R. Procopio, 31–39. Washington, DC: NAEYC.

Castro, D.C., E.E. García, & A.M. Markos. 2013. *Dual Language Learners: Research Informing Policy.* Chapel Hill: University of North Carolina, Frank Porter Graham Child Development Institute, Center for Early Care and Education—Dual Language Learners.

Christie, J.F., B.J. Enz, C. Vukelich, & K.A. Roskos. 2014. *Teaching Language and Literacy: Preschool Through the Elementary Grades.* 5th ed. New York: Pearson Education.

Copple, C., & S. Bredekamp, eds. 2009. *Developmentally Appropriate Practice in Ealy Childhood Programs from Birth Through Age 8.* 3rd ed. Washington, DC: NAEYC.

De Houwer, A. 2009. *Bilingual First Language Acquisition.* Bristol, UK: Multilingual Matters.

Durán, L. Forthcoming. "Building on the Strengths of Dual Language Learners with Disabilities." In *Advancing Equity in Early Childhood Education,* eds. I. Alanís & I.U. Iruka, with B. Willer & S. Friedman. Washington, DC: NAEYC.

Elicker, J., & M. Benson McMullan. 2013. "Appropriate and Meaningful Assessment in Family-Centered Programs." *Young Children* 68 (3): 22–27.

Espinosa, L.M. 2005. "Curriculum and Assessment Considerations for Young Children from Culturally, Linguistically, and Economically Diverse Backgrounds." *Psychology in the Schools* 42 (8): 837–53.

García, O., S. Ibarra Johnson, & K. Seltzer. 2017. *The Translanguaging Classroom: Leveraging Student Bilingualism for Learning.* Philadelphia: Caslon.

García, O., & T. Kleyn. 2016. *Translanguaging with Multilingual Students: Learning from Classroom Moments.* New York: Routledge.

García, O., & L. Wei. 2014. *Translanguaging: Language, Bilingualism, and Education.* New York: Palgrave Macmillan.

Gardner-Neblett, N., & I. Iruka. 2015. "Oral Narrative Skills: Explaining the Language-Emergent Literacy Link by Race/Ethnicity and SES." *Developmental Psychology* 51 (7): 889–904. doi:10.1037/a0039274.

Gibson, T., E. Peña, & L. Bedore. 2014. "The Relation Between Language Experience and Receptive-Expressive Semantic Gaps in Bilingual Children." *International Journal of Bilingual Education and Bilingualism* 17 (1): 90–110.

Gillanders, C., & L. Soltero-Gonzalez. 2019. "Discovering How Writing Works in Different Languages: Lessons from Dual Language Learners." *Young Children* 74 (2): 14–23.

Guiberson, M., & K.P. Ferris. 2019. "Early Language Interventions for Young Dual Language Learners: A Scoping Review." *American Journal of Speech-Language Pathology* 28 (3): 945–63.

Hornberger, N.H. 1992. "Biliteracy Contexts, Continua, and Contrasts: Policy and Curriculum for Cambodian and Puerto Rican Students in Philadelphia." *Education and Urban Society* 24 (2): 196–211.

Krashen, S.D. 1982. *Principles and Practices in Second Language Acquisition.* Oxford: Pergamon Press.

Kroeger, J., & T. Cardy. 2006. "Documentation: A Hard to Reach Place." *Early Childhood Education Journal* 33 (6): 389–98. doi:10.1007/s10643-006-0062-6.

Michael-Luna, S. 2013. "What Linguistically Diverse Parents Know and How It Can Help Early Childhood Educators: A Case Study of a Dual Language Preschool Community." *Early Childhood Education Journal* 41 (6): 447–455.

Mindes, G., & L.A. Jung. 2015. *Assessing Young Children.* 5th ed. Upper Saddle River, NJ: Pearson.

Moreno, A.J., & M.M. Klute. 2011. "Infant-Toddler Teachers Can Successfully Employ Authentic Assessment: The Learning Through Relating System." *Early Childhood Research Quarterly* 26 (4): 484–96.

NASEM (National Academies of Sciences, Engineering, and Medicine). 2017. *Promoting the Educational Success of Children and Youth Learning English: Promising Futures.* Washington, DC: National Academies Press. doi:10.17226/24677.

Paradis, J. 2010. "The Interface Between Bilingual Development and Specific Language Impairment." *Applied Psycholinguistics* 31 (2): 227–52.

Paradis, J., F. Genesee, & M.B. Crago. 2011. *Dual Language Development and Disorders. A Handbook on Bilingualism and Second Language Learning.* 2nd ed. Baltimore: Brookes.

Place, S., & E. Hoff. 2011. "Properties of Dual Language Exposure that Influence 2-Year-Old's Bilingual Proficiency." *Child Development* 82 (6): 1834–49.

Roberts, T. 2014. "Not So Silent After All: Examination and Analysis of the Silent Stage in Childhood Second Language Acquisition." *Early Childhood Research Quarterly* 29 (1): 22–40.

Roller, S.A., E.P. Cunningham, & K.A. Marin. 2019. "Photographs and Learning Progressions: Supports for Intentional Assessment and Instruction in Mathematics." *Young Children* 74 (3): 26–33.

Rueda, R., & J. Stillman. 2012. "The 21st Century Teacher: A Cultural Perspective." *Journal of Teacher Education* 63: 245–53.

Seitz, H. 2008. "The Power of Documentation in the Early Childhood Classroom." *Young Children* 36 (1): 88–93.

Shabazian, A.N. 2016. "The Role of Documentation in Fostering Learning." *Young Children* 71 (3): 73–79.

Vygotsky, L.S. 1978. *Mind in Society: The Development of Higher Psychological Processes.* Cambridge: Harvard University Press.

Yun, S. 2008. "Role-Play and Language Socialization Among Bilingual Korean Children in the United States." *Simulation Gaming* 39 (2): 240–52.

naeyc®
Accreditation
Early Learning Programs

This chapter supports the following NAEYC Early Learning Program Accreditation Standards and topic areas:

Standard 4: Assessment of Child Progress

4.A Creating an Assessment Plan

4.B Using Appropriate Assessment Methods

4.C Identifying Children's Interests and Needs and Describing Children's Progress

4.D Adapting Curriculum, Individualizing Teaching, and Informing Program Development

4.E Communicating with Families and Involving Families in the Assessment Process

9 A Glimpse into Ms. Rocha's Classroom: An Integrated Lesson

Objectives

> Discuss how to integrate listening, speaking, reading, and writing into daily activities.

> Explain how children's natural curiosity promotes language development.

> Illustrate how concrete experiences provide opportunities for conceptual development.

> Identify activities for learning that relate to your curriculum.

Ms. Rocha is the English model teacher in a Spanish–English dual language classroom. She teaches science in English, and her teaching partner teaches other subjects in Spanish. Ms. Rocha's dual language prekindergartners have been busy learning about the fall season. Children have read and written about pumpkins, discussed various family activities, and identified characteristics of the season. Ms. Rocha invited families to send various objects found in nature from their homes and communities. Throughout the week, the children explore the various items (e.g., rocks, leaves, acorns, twigs, pumpkins) and are excited to go on a leaf hunt.

In this chapter, we peek into Ms. Rocha's prekindergarten classroom to see how she activates children's previous knowledge, engages children in social interactions, augments children's oral and written vocabulary through comprehensible input, and develops concepts across the content areas. The glimpses of instruction we capture illustrate how teachers can integrate listening, speaking, reading, and writing through language-rich activities, such as read-alouds, morning messages, nature walks, and journal writing. During Phase 1 of an interdisciplinary biliteracy sequence of learning (see Chapter 6), Ms. Rocha begins with concrete experiences and actively involves learners in discussions about tangible objects—in this case, leaves. We explore how Ms. Rocha integrates the science topic of leaves throughout her learning centers so that children can continue discovering, talking, and learning about the concepts in all content areas.

The three phases of the integrated learning sequence Ms. Rocha used in her prekindergarten classroom, including other books and activities, may be found in Appendix A.

Morning Arrival

As children arrive to the classroom, Ms. Rocha stands at the door and greets them with smiles and hugs. She says, "Good morning, Ana! How are you today? Good morning, Jorge!" Children's responses vary. Some say, "Good morning, Ms. Rocha!" while some just say, "Good morning," and others simply smile. Children hang their backpacks in the spaces marked by their names and move their picture on a T-chart to reflect "Who is at school?" and "Who is at home?" Children then move to the circular carpet to start their day. While on the carpet, they quietly talk to each other, adjust their shoes, or twirl their hair.

Ms. Rocha plays a song: "Hello, friend, how are you? I'm very happy to see you." Children stand up and begin to sing and dance to the familiar tune. The song specifically asks children to engage with a peer as they "greet their neighbor (with a handshake), give a bump and turn around." Ms. Rocha participates in the morning greeting along with the children; she smiles, giggles, and happily greets each child.

Morning Message

Children resettle on the carpet and sit next to their bilingual partner. Ms. Rocha sits in front of the children and says, "Okay, let's get started with our morning message." She writes, *Today we will go on a leaf hunt.* As she writes, she enunciates each word and emphasizes certain sounds (*F* in *leaf* and *T* in *hunt*). Once she is done writing, she asks the children to read the sentence with her. She then asks them to "see how many words are in the sentence." Children count along with her. As she reads each word, she writes the corresponding number under each word. Children call out, "We have eight words!"

Ms. Rocha then directs her class of 4-year-olds to look outside. She asks, "What do you think the weather will be like when we go on our hunt?" Children look out the window, and several say it will be sunny. Ms. Rocha agrees and augments what they said with, "I think it is going to be a nice sunny fall day." She begins to write the sentence but stops after the word *nice*. She gestures to Sara, a native Spanish speaker, and asks if she would like to help write the next word, *sunny*. Sara smiles as she takes the marker from Ms. Rocha. Ms. Rocha asks Sara to listen to the initial sound of the word, emphasizing the *S* sound. Sara repeats after her, producing the *S* sound. Ms. Rocha validates her attempt: "That's right. It's an *S* sound, so it's the letter . . . ?" Sara, softly replies, "*S*."

Ms. Rocha smiles and motions for Sara to write the letter on the chart paper. Sara writes a large capital *S*. Ms. Rocha completes the word for Sara. Again, she asks children to read the sentence she just wrote. Ms. Rocha then asks children to think about how many leaves they might find on their leaf hunt. Children call out various responses and agree on at least three for each pair of children. With each step of the shared writing process, Ms. Rocha has children reread what she has written and discuss what they might write next. After they complete their morning message, Ms. Rocha plays a video for the children called "How Many Leaves?" The video shows a tree with three leaves in red, yellow, and green. She asks children to count the leaves and then identify their colors. Children sing along.

An Interdisciplinary Biliteracy Sequence: Collecting Leaves!

Nothing happens at random in this classroom. As children get ready for their nature walk, they look at their bilingual pairs list to see who their assigned partner will be for their leaf hunt and quickly find their nature walk partner. Before stepping outside, Ms. Rocha announces, "Let's go outside to explore and collect some leaves. Remember your senses? We will use our five senses to explore and collect leaves." Ms. Rocha shows children a picture of all the senses and has them repeat after her as they point to their eyes, nose, ears, hands, and mouth while she says, "Sight, smell, hearing, touch, and taste."

To ensure children understand her expectations, Ms. Rocha provides concrete instructions:

"First, we will observe and collect three leaves: small, medium, and large. Then we will collect three leaves of different colors. Finally, you will find one leaf that you love so much you want to use it to make art." Ms. Rocha brings an anchor chart in a folder that outlines the three required steps, including visuals to remind children during their walk.

Children know to remain with their partner, share materials, and help each other complete the activity. They receive only one plastic sealable bag and one hand lens to observe the leaves closely. They take turns collecting the leaves. After Ana finds one leaf that is small, she gives the plastic bag to Carlos so that she can find a medium-sized leaf. Then Ana locates a larger leaf, and with that they have completed the first step. Ms. Rocha observes and

compliments them: "What a great job! You found dry oak leaves of three different sizes: small, medium, and large. You are now ready for step two." Then another pair lets her know that they have found three leaves of different colors. She asks the children, "Wow! Where did you find these maroon, ochre, and yellow leaves?" "Over by the tree!" says one of the children.

In about 15 minutes, everyone has collected at least three leaves, including one they love. They are ready to come back and talk about their experience. Ms. Rocha gathers everyone on the carpet and begins a language experience approach (see Chapter 6). As part of this approach, she asks children to narrate their experience ("What did we just do?") and she writes their words. Voices begin to emerge, and Ms. Rocha transcribes a message as shown in Figure 9.1.

Ms. Rocha will use this message to continue with the lesson tomorrow. In the meantime, she has identified a book for a read-aloud that will allow children to extend and validate their current knowledge of leaves, classification, objects in nature, and language labels related to it.

Read-Aloud

Ms. Rocha transitions to a read-aloud that integrates literacy and science with repetitive text: *We're Going on a Leaf Hunt,* by Steve Metzger. She engages in a dialogic reading strategy where she pauses to ask open-ended questions and emphasizes selected vocabulary (e.g., *over, around, across*). While reading, Ms. Rocha encourages children to act out the story with the book characters. They pretend to climb a hill, step into a

---

Today we took a nature walk looking for leaves

With our partners, we walked outside and found small, medium, and large leaves. There were a lot of leaves, so it was easy!

Next, we found leaves in different colors: yellow, brown, green, orange, and maroon.

Finally, we found a pretty leaf that we love. We had fun!

Figure 9.1. Morning message.

forest, slide through a waterfall, and row a boat as they act out looking for leaves. She also identifies vocabulary words for her word wall (e.g., *squish, splash, skunk*) and asks children to repeat words with her (e.g., *row, row, plip, plop*). As the book ends, she has children turn and talk to their neighbor about who they think is hiding behind that bush. Children look at the picture and excitedly predict a skunk, a cat, or a bear. Children squeal and wrinkle their noses when they discover it is a black-and-white skunk!

Once finished with the read-aloud, Ms. Rocha refers children to the board where she has written a sentence stem: "I found _____." She asks children to tell her what kind of leaves they found in their nature walk. She holds up several leaves, and children indicate, "brown leaves," "rainbow leaves," "three leaves," "small leaves," "lots of leaves." She writes each of their responses. She also scaffolds children's language during this process by questioning them on their leaf finds. When Selina states that she found "rainbow leaves," Ms. Rocha encourages her to talk about her leaves by saying, "What can you tell me about your rainbow leaves?" Selina proudly holds one of her leaves and points to the various color tones found on it. Ms. Rocha responds, "Wow that is an interesting find! Your leaf is multicolored. It has brown, yellow, and ochre tones." Selina smiles and repeats, "Yes, brown, yellow, and ochre." Finally, Ms. Rocha reads the children's responses and tells them to choose what they would like to add to their journals. Children take out their daily journals and draw or write about the different leaves they found. They refer to the words written on the board to help them complete the writing task. When they complete their drawings or writings, children share what they created with their partner.

Using Songs, Modeling, and Visual Cues to Facilitate Transitions and Routines

Ms. Rocha cheerfully begins to sing her usual learning center transition song to the familiar tune of "The Farmer in the Dell": "We're going to the centers, we're going to the centers, hi-ho, the derry-o, we're going to the centers. We're putting journals away, we're putting journals away, hi-ho, the derry-o, we're putting journals away." As children hear the transition song, they join in the singing and start returning their journals to the blue basket labeled Journals and sit on the edge of the carpet. Ms. Rocha understands that transitions can be difficult for young children, who do not adapt well to change. She also understands that dual language learners might not yet understand the words in the song, so she models putting journals away and involves them in the process as they sing along. The consistent use of a transition song creates an auditory scaffold for children to transition to their next activity.

Ms. Rocha then calls on Luis, the schedule helper, to walk to the front of the class. Children in her classroom are attentive to the visual cue of the schedule to see what activity is next. Luis changes the clothespin on the schedule to the picture that illustrates the next major transition—children working in learning centers. Together, Luis and Ms. Rocha read the print "Learning centers." Other children read the print as well and get excited over learning center time. Ms. Rocha thanks Luis for helping read the schedule. She understands the importance of having a regular schedule with visuals that guide DLLs through the day.

Several children then ask Ms. Rocha if they can help her get the "surprise box." This is a box with *Surprise Box* written in blue print in English on one side and *Caja Sorpresa* in red print in Spanish on the other side. The box holds new learning center activities or games that she will introduce for the day or week. However, Luis reminds everyone that this is Patricia's classroom duty as he points to her picture and name on the classroom helpers chart. "You're right, Luis. It's Patricia's duty," says Ms. Rocha, who also points to her name on the chart. Patricia is excited to help move the box to the carpet area and to find out what is in the box. Patricia opens the box and pulls out a bag of leaves (from the leaf hunt), bottles of paint, and white paper. Ms. Rocha uses verbal mapping to describe a new learning center activity (leaf prints) for the art center as she points to a task card. She uses task cards with illustrations and color-coded words to guide children's independence while at their learning centers.

Learning Centers

Ms. Rocha understands young children's natural desire to play and how it contributes to their development, but most importantly, she understands how learning through play lowers the affective filter of DLLs. Therefore, she has carefully selected games, materials, and resources for the learning centers with the goal of enhancing children's language and academic learning through various domains. The learning centers have a variety of multisensory activities to meet the diverse needs and interests of children in her classroom. All activities revolve around the topic of leaves. Let's peek into some of her learning centers.

Writing Center

This center has a shelf with a variety of writing materials, papers, and other resources labeled in English and Spanish that support emergent writers. Ms. Rocha knows that preschoolers have diverse interests and needs when it comes to writing. Therefore, she has prepared a variety of developmentally appropriate writing activities for children to select. The first basket has playdough and word cards with pictures based on their recent leaf hunt. Using the playdough, children are forming words such as *leaves, ground, crunchy leaves, dancing leaves,* and *oak tree.* In the second basket, Ms. Rocha included blank books titled *My Leaf Book* to encourage children to write about their experience during their nature walk. DLLs are very diverse and express themselves in unique ways. Some children scribble, while others draw to communicate. Some form letter strings, a few use the words from their word walls, and some write phrases about their experience. A couple might even write whole sentences. Nevertheless, when Ms. Rocha asks them to share what they have authored with their partners, they all have detailed stories to tell! As they tell their stories, she audio-records them to help her assess their oral narrative skills.

The third basket reflects her knowledge about the importance of culture in children's lives. Ms. Rocha added another blank book titled *Leaves I Eat at Home* with a word bank in English and Spanish that she created with the children after their science lesson on edible leaves. The fourth basket has a sentence stem that says "A leaf_____" and a plastic bag securely taped and filled with finger paint for children to describe their finds from the nature walk. Children enjoyed writing and erasing on the taped plastic bag. Some of the words they used to describe their leaves included *crunchy, brown, yellow, rainbow,* and *orange.* By the end of the week, most children could read and write the sentence stem through this scaffolded writing activity.

Art Center

The art center has been set up as a place where children express themselves through a variety of media. It is located next to the classroom sink and close to the writing center. It also has a bulletin board labeled Our Art Gallery/Nuestra galería de arte with a collection of children's artwork displayed along with various art supplies. She labeled supplies in English and Spanish and included crayons, markers, watercolors, paints, a variety of paper, and other materials used for art creation. This week, it also includes leaves children collected during their leaf hunt. As in the other learning centers, there are four children in this area. Two are brushing their leaves with paint and two are making leaf prints.

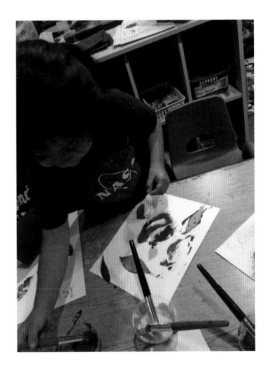

They are excited to see the prints on their paper, and they start comparing their creations. "*¡Mira!*" (Look!) says Vanessa as she points to the vein markings the leaf left on her paper. "*¡Mira, el mío tiene más rayitas!*" (Look, mine has more lines), says Yesenia. When Ms. Rocha hears this, she approaches them and asks, "Which leaf left the most

vein markings?" as she points to the two leaves and the leaf veins. The girls start counting each other's vein markings on their papers and engage in a discussion about their leaves.

The other two children at the center decide to make "leaf creations" by gluing leaves on a white paper with the sentence stem "A leaf _____." "I'm making a leaf monster," Joaquin says aloud. Ms. Rocha approaches Joaquin and asks him to describe his leaf monster. Joaquin responds, "It's a big leaf monster that eats leaves." Ms. Rocha asks, "Why did you decide to create a leaf monster?" Joaquin smiles and responds, "I thinking of the good monster on TV." She then turns to Emilio, who is very focused on his creation. Once he is done, she asks, "Emilio, what can you tell me about your creation?" Emilio says, "I made a leaf pattern, look!" Ms. Rocha acknowledges his work: "Wow, I see your pattern! Small leaf, big leaf, small leaf, big leaf, an AB pattern." Emilio then asks Ms. Rocha to help him spell the word *pattern*. Before leaving, she takes pictures of their creations to share with their families.

After carefully observing children in the art center and noticing that they are still enthused by using leaves as an art medium, Ms. Rocha decides to introduce a leaf collage. She has noticed that DLLs in her class enjoy communicating through their art creations. She uses this informal assessment to further scaffold their oral language as she encourages them to talk with each other about their creations.

For further ideas on how Ms. Rocha extended opportunities for DLLs to explore the topic of leaves in other centers, please see Appendix B: Fall Theme: Learning Objectives and Learning Centers at the end of the chapter. You will see how Ms. Rocha intentionally plans opportunities for children to develop their language, literacy, across content areas.

What Does This Mean?

Congruent with NAEYC's goal to improve the quality and equitable practices of early learning programs for young children, this book focused on ways to respond to the needs of children from homes where English is not the primary language of communication (NAEYC 2009, 2019). NAEYC urges educators to recognize the socioemotional toll on young children when they are immersed in educational settings that ignore their language and their culture.

With this in mind, the glimpse into Ms. Rocha's prekindergarten classroom contextualized learning and presented an overview of ways in which lesson design can provide equal access to high-quality instruction. This chapter reveals the many ways in which the teacher designed every instructional moment, including arrival, learning sequence, transitions, routines, and learning center time, using current research from the field of early childhood and bilingual education.

Building Relationships

Ms. Rocha recognized the crucial role that emotional well-being plays in learning. As we know, children learn best when they feel welcome and valued. Ms. Rocha took specific steps to ensure this, including standing by the door greeting children by name and smiling as they entered the classroom. This greeting moment influences learning in significant ways. First, it contributes to the development of positive relationships between teacher and children. Second, it positions the teacher as a model of social-informal language. Finally, it establishes predictable routines, which in this case included singing a song, making time to socialize with each other, and preparing for learning.

Placing Language, Culture, and Family at the Center of an Interdisciplinary Biliteracy Sequence

Language

Whether a lesson is conducted in English (as illustrated in Ms. Rocha's classroom) or in children's home language, early childhood educators recognize the benefits of engaging children in a learning sequence that begins with concrete opportunities to explore and discover. It is in the context of concrete, direct experiences that language ceases to be an abstract tool and becomes a relevant resource as children listen, speak, and construct meaning. Additionally, Ms. Rocha continuously made oral language visible in the form of written morning messages, anchor charts, transcriptions of children's accounts after the walk, and word walls. Exposure to language in relation to curricular objectives is also extended as children participate in learning centers that invite new forms of expression. She creates spaces where children can expand their linguistic repertoires by utilizing their multimodal and multilingual resources as assets in their learning.

Culture and Family

Ms. Rocha understands the need to design instruction that is culturally responsive and connected to children's previous knowledge. She purposefully invited families to share resources found at home or in their community. She then used these resources as part of children's learning. Additionally, she added a blank book titled *Leaves I Eat at Home* to her writing center. This opens spaces for self-expression and discussion of cultural practices in children's families. Encouraging children to share their stories with each other creates opportunities to talk, learn, and develop positive cross-cultural perspectives and appreciation of the ways in which each of them is unique. Together they create a shared social world (Genishi & Dyson 2009).

Content

Teachers who are responsive to the cultural and linguistic makeup of their learners know that they must also prioritize cognitive engagement. Ms. Rocha understands her responsibility to develop children's academic language and skills in a playful manner that is rooted in their everyday experiences. She helps children draw from their cultural knowledge and apply it to broader disciplinary contexts. Ms. Rocha knows that much of the academic vocabulary that she needs to introduce will be new to all children regardless of their assigned label as "English proficient" or "Spanish proficient." This is why she makes sure that all the language she produces is comprehensible and always accompanied by visuals, gestures, realia, and clear tone of voice. She encourages children to talk about science concepts through reciprocal conversations, shared writing, and partner-based learning. As they do, she informally assesses language choice and communicative function.

Summary

Supporting DLLs in their learning trajectories requires intentional pedagogies that address children's socioemotional, cognitive, and language needs. Teachers like Ms. Rocha see the wealth of knowledge DLLs bring to the classroom. They use this knowledge to further children's academic and linguistic development. However, there is also a strong focus on helping children feel connected to others within a community of learners. The development of children's socioemotional well-being is a crucial part of teaching, "for one cannot learn without feeling secure in one's own identity and performances" (García, Ibarra Johnson, and Seltzer 2017, 157). Ultimately, our goal is to support DLLs on their journey toward becoming bilingual, biliterate, and bicultural citizens who can critically navigate and transform their academic and social worlds.

Key Points to Remember!

> Use current research from the field of early childhood and bilingual education when designing instructional moments, including arrival, learning sequence, transitions, routines, and learning center time.

> The emotional well-being of all children plays a crucial role in how and what they learn.

> Whether a lesson is conducted in English (as illustrated in Ms. Rocha's classroom) or in children's home language, early childhood educators recognize the benefits of engaging children in a learning sequence that begins with concrete opportunities to explore and discover.

> Make oral language visible in the form of written morning messages, anchor charts, transcriptions of children's accounts, and word walls. Exposure to language in relation to curricular objectives is also extended as children participate in learning centers that invite new forms of expression.

> It is important to design instruction that is culturally responsive and connected to children's previous knowledge.

> Teachers who are responsive to the cultural and linguistic makeup of their learners know that they must also prioritize cognitive engagement.

References

García, O., S. Ibarra Johnson, & K. Seltzer. 2017. *The Translanguaging Classroom: Leveraging Student Bilingualism for Learning*. Philadelphia: Caslon.

Genishi, C., & A.H. Dyson. 2009. *Children Language and Literacy: Diverse Learners in Diverse Times*. New York: Teachers College Press.

NAEYC. 2009. "Where We Stand on Responding to Linguistic and Cultural Diversity." Position statement supplement. Washington, DC: NAEYC. www.naeyc.org/files/naeyc/file/positions/diversity.pdf.

NAEYC. 2019. "Advancing Equity in Early Childhood Education." Position statement. Washington, DC: NAEYC. www.naeyc.org/resources/position-statements/equity.

naeyc®
Accreditation
Early Learning Programs

This chapter supports the following NAEYC Early Learning Program Accreditation Standards and topic areas:

Standard 1: Relationships
1.B Building Positive Relationships Between Teachers and Children

Standard 2: Curriculum
2.B Social and Emotional Development
2.D Language Development
2.E Early Literacy
2.F Early Mathematics
2.G Science
2.L Social Studies

Appendix A: Integrated Learning Sequence

Phase 1

Nature walk: Collecting leaves

Materials:

- Bag
- Hand lens

Procedure:

- Collaborate with a partner.
- Collect three leaves of different sizes.
- Collect three leaves of different colors.
- Choose one leaf that you think is beautiful.

Phase 2

- Language experience activity.

Phase 3

- Read-aloud: We're Going on a Leaf Hunt, by Steve Metzger
- Sentence stem: I found_____.

Books for This Theme or Lesson

At the Farmers Market/En el mercado, by Anna W. Bardaus

Fall Leaves: Colorful and Crunchy, by Martha E.H. Rustad

Fletcher and the Falling Leaves, by Julia Rawlinson

The Giving Tree, by Shel Silverstein

Goodbye Summer, Hello Autumn, by Kenard Pak

Leaf Jumpers, by Carole Gerber

Leaf Man, by Lois Ehlert

Leaves, by David Ezra Stein

Leaves, by Vijaya Khisty Bodach

Leaves Fall Down: Learning About Autumn Leaves, by Lisa Marie Bullard

Plants Feed Me, by Lizzy Rockwell

Red Leaf, Yellow Leaf, by Lois Ehlert

There Was an Old Lady Who Swallowed Some Leaves! by Lucille Colandro

We're Going on a Leaf Hunt, by Steve Metzger

Yellow Time, by Lauren Stringer

Additional Leaf Activities and Lessons

Leaf Activities for Young Learners: www.plt.org/educator-tips/leaf-activities-young-learners

Look at Those Leaves! http://sciencenetlinks.com/lessons/look-at-those-leaves

Leaf Activities for Preschoolers: https://teachingmama.org/8-leaf-activities-for-preschoolers

Appendix B: Fall Theme
Learning Objectives and Learning Centers

Learning Objectives: Fall Theme	
Science Objective ❯ Children observe, investigate, describe, and discuss leaves and their properties and uses. ❯ Children classify and sort leaves that are the same and different into groups, and they use language to describe how the groups are similar and different.	**Social Studies Objective** ❯ Children identify and compare similarities and differences among the leaves they found and how they use leaves at home.
Art Objective ❯ Children use a variety of art materials and activities for sensory experience and exploration with leaves.	**Mathematics Objective** ❯ Children demonstrate that the order of the counting sequence is always the same, regardless of what is counted (e.g., leaves, twigs, rocks). ❯ Children recognize and compare widths or lengths of leaves. ❯ Children collect and sort leaves on a floor graph.
Emergent Literacy Objective ❯ Children engage in free-drawing and writing activities related to fall. ❯ Children intentionally use marks, letters, or symbols to record language and verbally share meaning about their experiences with the new topic they are studying.	**Language Objective** ❯ Children use a wide variety of words to label and describe their experiences with leaves. ❯ Children combine sentences that give a lot of detail, stick to the topic, and clearly communicate intended meaning. ❯ Children use math vocabulary such as pattern, sort, and category.

Fall Theme Ideas for Additional Learning Centers

Library Center

Materials included:

> Rug, beanbags, and small table

> Variety of writing tools and paper

> Books in English and Spanish related to the topic (see list below)

> Stuffed animals with bilingual sign that says Read to Us and Leenos

Activities

> Teacher-made felt board with felt pieces that connected to the *How Many Leaves* video

> "Las hojas bailaban" ("The Leaves Were Dancing") Spanish rhyme chart with pointer

> Self-recorded stories for children to listen to and follow along

> Box with bilingual title Interesting Words/Palabras Interesantes with magnifying glass, index cards, and markers for children to find words in books and place on the word wall

Math Center

Materials included:

> Table

> Floor space

> Baskets labeled in two languages with activity choices

> Books related to the topic

Activities

> Basket 1: Seriating a collection of leaves

> Basket 2: Graphing leaves with a shower curtain as a floor graph

> Basket 3: Picture puzzles of children's neighborhood surrounded by leaves

> Basket 4: Forming patterns with leaves

> Basket 5: Math books

> Basket 6: Unifix cubes and leaves (brought from home) to measure leaves

Science Center

Materials included:

> Variety of leaves

> Magnifying glasses

> Pumpkins of various sizes

> Sorting trays

> Books related to topic

Activities

> Basket 1: Sort and classify leaves brought from home and leaves from the leaf hunt

> Basket 2: Drop and compare how long it takes falling leaves to reach the floor; provide leaves and timer

> Basket 3: Scented jars with leaves (donated by families) used for cooking (e.g., cilantro, parsley, basil)

Construction Center

Materials included:

> Variety of blocks

> Construction resources and accessories (e.g., signs, artificial leaves, plastic rake, vehicles)

> Writing tools (markers, crayons, pencils)

> Index cards, tape, sticky notes, variety of paper

> Tongue depressors and clay

> Photo albums with pictures of children's communities

> Books related to topic

> Environmental print signs

Fall Theme Ideas for Additional Learning Centers

Science Center, cont. 〉 Basket 4: Make a salad following a task card (with illustrations) using edible leaves (e.g., spinach, lettuce, cabbage, kale) 〉 Basket 5: Graph "leaves we eat" using sticky notes and wall graph 〉 Basket 6: Sensory box with items from their nature walk	
Dramatic Play Center Create a plant nursery and label it Classroom Nursery Materials included: 〉 Pots, Styrofoam, artificial leaves, and flowers 〉 Potting soil bag, fertilizer boxes, bags of seeds (or other empty bags of resources needed at a plant nursery) 〉 Plastic gardening tools (e.g., bucket, shovel, rake, hoe, watering can) 〉 Small wagon to move plants 〉 Aprons and gloves Include authentic literacy props such as: 〉 Signs that say things like "Caution Wet Floor" and "Open/Closed," receipt booklet, writing tools and paper Create an album with pictures of plants and leaves found in their community and include their names.	**What other centers might enhance language and literacy opportunities in Ms. Rocha's class?**

Additional Resources

Assessment

Halle, T., M. Zaslow, J. Wessel, S. Moodie, & K. Darling-Churchill. 2011. *Understanding and Choosing Assessments and Developmental Screeners for Young Children Ages 3–5: Profiles of Selected Measures*. Report. Washington, DC: Office of Planning, Research, and Evaluation, Administration for Children and Families, US. Department of Health and Human Services. https://eclkc.ohs.acf.hhs .gov/child-screening-assessment/article /understanding-choosing-assessments -developmental-screeners-young.

Office of Head Start. n.d. "Gathering and Using Language Information that Families Share." https://eclkc.ohs.acf.hhs.gov/sites/default /files/pdf/gathering-using-language-info -families-share.pdf.

Classroom Strategies

Center for Applied Linguistics. n.d. "Sheltered Instruction Observation Protocol." http://cal.org/siop.

National Center on Cultural and Linguistic Responsiveness. 2015. *Classroom Language Models: A Leaders' Implementation Manual*. Report prepared for the US Department of Health and Human Services, Administration for Children and Families, Office of Head Start. Washington, DC: US Department of Health and Human Services, Administration for Children and Families, Office of Head Start. https:// eclkc.ohs.acf.hhs.gov/sites/default/files/pdf /pps-language-models.pdf.

Office of Head Start. 2019. "Specific Strategies to Support DLLs When Adults Do Not Speak Their Language," last modified December 13. https:// eclkc.ohs.acf.hhs.gov/culture-language/article /specific-strategies-support-dual-language -learners-dlls-when-adults-do-not-speak-their -language.

Developing Language and Literacy

Chapman de Sousa, E.B. 2019. "Five Tips for Engaging Multilingual Children in Conversation." *Young Children* 74 (2): 23–31.

Copple, C., S. Bredekamp, D. Koralek, & K. Charner, eds. 2013. *Developmentally Appropriate Practice: Focus on Preschoolers*. Washington, DC: NAEYC.

Folsom, J.S. 2017. "Dialogic Reading: Having a Conversation About Books." *Iowa Reading Research Center* (blog), January 3. https:// iowareadingresearch.org/blog/dialogic -reading-having-a-conversation-about-books. (posted in multiple languages)

Shidler, L. 2012. "Teaching Vocabulary in Preschool: Teachers, Children, Families." *Teaching Young Children* 5 (3): 13–15.

Dual Language Education

Arreguín-Anderson, M.G., & I. Alanís. 2019. *Translingual Partners in Early Childhood Elementary-Education: Pedagogies on Linguistic and Cognitive Engagement.* New York: Peter Lang Publishing.

Collier, V., & W. Thomas. 2009. *Educating English Language Learners for a Transformed World.* Albuquerque, NM: Fuente Press.

Colorín Colorado. n.d. "ELL Glossary." www .colorincolorado.org/ell-basics/ell-glossary.

Dombrink-Green, M., H. Bohart, & K. Nemeth. 2014. *Spotlight on Young Children: Supporting Dual Language Learners.* Washington, DC: NAEYC.

Ferlazzo, L., & K.H. Sypnieski. 2018. *The ELL Teacher's Toolbox: Hundreds of Practical Ideas to Support Your Students.* New Jersey: Jossey Bass.

Hammer, C., E. Hoff, Y. Uchikoshi, C. Gillanders, D. Castro, & L. Sandilos. 2014. "The Language and Literacy Development of Young Dual Language Learners: A Critical Review." *Early Childhood Research Quarterly* 29 (4): 715–33.

Howard, E.R., K.J. Lindholm-Leary, D. Rogers, N. Olague, J. Medina, B. Kennedy, J. Sugarman, & D. Christian. 2018. *Guiding Principles for Dual Language Education.* 3rd ed. Washington, DC: Center for Applied Linguistics; Albuquerque, NM: Dual Language Education of New Mexico; Miami, FL: Santillana USA.

Koralek, D., ed. 2013. Supporting Dual Language Learners and Their Families [issue cluster topic]. *Young Children* 68 (1).

NASEM (National Academies of Sciences, Engineering, and Medicine). 2017. *Promoting the Educational Success of Children and Youth Learning English: Promising Futures.* Washington, DC: National Academies Press. doi:10.17226/24677.

National Center on Cultural and Linguistic Responsiveness. n.d. "Same, Different, and Diverse: Understanding Children Who Are Dual Language Learners." Report prepared for the US Department of Health and Human Services, Administration for Children and Families, Office of Head Start. Washington, DC: US Department of Health and Human Services, Administration for Children and Families, Office of Head Start. https://eclkc.ohs.acf.hhs .gov/sites/default/files/pdf/research-same -different-diverse-eng.pdf.

Nemeth, K. 2016. *Young Dual Language Learners: A Guide for PreK–3 Leaders.* Philadelphia: Caslon Publishing.

Nemeth, K. 2013. *Basics of Supporting Dual Language Learners: An Introduction for Educators of Children from Birth through Age 8.* Washington, DC: NAEYC.

Nemeth, K. 2009. *Many Languages, One Classroom: Teaching Dual and English Language Learners.* Lewisville, NC: Gryphon House. Includes tips and techniques for preschool teachers.

Office of Head Start. 2020. "Dual Language Learners Toolkit," last modified March 9. https://eclkc.ohs.acf.hhs.gov/culture-language /article/dual-language-learners-toolkit.

Steele, J.L., R. Slater, G. Zamarro, T. Miller, J.J. Li, S. Burkhauser, & M. Bacon. 2017. "Dual-Language Immersion Programs Raise Student Achievement in English." (Research Brief No.9903). Santa Monica, CA: RAND Corporation. www.rand.org/pubs/research _briefs/RB9903.html.

DLLs with Disabilities

Brillante, P. 2017. *The Essentials: Supporting Young Children with Disabilities in the Classroom.* Washington DC: NAEYC.

Hamayan, E., B. Marler, C. Sánchez-López, & J. Damico. 2013. *Special Education Considerations for English Language Learners: Delivering a Continuum of Services.* 2nd ed. Philadelphia: Caslon Publishers.

Hansel, L., ed. 2019. Intentional and Supportive: Appropriate Uses of Early Assessments [issue cluster topic]. *Young Children* 74 (3).

NAEYC. 2013. *Classroom-Based Assessment of Preschoolers: An Introduction to What Teachers Need to Know. Trainer's Manual.* Washington, DC: NAEYC.

Ray, J.A., J. Pweitt-Kinder, & S. George. 2009. "Partnering with Families of Children with Special Needs." *Young Children* 64 (5): 16–22.

Shillady, A., ed. 2013. Using Documentation and Assessment to Support Children's Learning [issue cluster topic]. *Young Children* 68 (3).

Simon-Cereijido, G., & V.F. Gutierrez-Clellen. 2014. "Bilingual Education for All: Latino Dual Language Learners with Language Disabilities." *International Journal of Bilingual Education and Bilingualism* 17 (2): 235–54.

Elements of Bilingualism

CUNY-NYS Initiative on Emergent Bilinguals: www.cuny-nysieb.org

Hansel, L., ed. 2019. Cultivating Bilingualism: The Benefits of Multilingual Classrooms [issue cluster topic]. *Young Children* 74 (2).

Office of Head Start. 2019. "Code Switching: Why It Matters and How to Respond," last modified February 4. https://eclkc.ohs.acf.hhs.gov /culture-language/article/code-switching-why -it-matters-how-respond.

Engaging Families

Breiseth, L., K. Robertson, & S. Lafond. 2015. "A Guide for Engaging ELL Families: Twenty Strategies for School Leaders." Colorín Colorado. www.colorincolorado.org/article /introduction-strategies-engaging-ell-families.

Cheatham, G.A., & R.M. Santos. 2011. "Collaborating with Families from Diverse Cultural and Linguistic Backgrounds: Considering Time and Communication Orientations." *Young Children* 66 (5): 76–83.

Global Family Research Project: www.hfrp.org

NAEYC's For Families: families.NAEYC.org

Teaching for Change. 2016. *Between Families and Schools: Creating Meaningful Relationships.* 2nd ed. Washington, DC: Teaching for Change.

Immigration

American Immigration Council. 2016. "Fact Sheet: Public Education for Immigrant Students: Understanding Plyler v. Doe." www.americanimmigrationcouncil.org /research/plyler-v-doe-public-education -immigrant-students.

Colorín Colorado. n.d. "Serving and Supporting Immigrant Students: Information for Schools." www.colorincolorado.org/ell-basics/serving -and-supporting-immigrant-students -information-schools.

University of California, UCLA. n.d. "The Civil Rights Project." www.civilrightsproject.ucla .edu/research/immigration.

Multicultural Children's Books

Center for the Study of Multicultural Children's Literature: www.csmcl.org

Clegg, L.B., E. Miller, B. Vanderhoof, G. Ramirez, & P.K. Ford. n.d. "How to Choose Outstanding Multicultural Books." *Scholastic Teacher.* www .scholastic.com/teachers/articles/teaching -content/how-choose-best-multicultural-books.

Derman-Sparks, L. n.d. "Guide for Selecting Anti-Bias Children's Books." *Social Justice Books.* https://socialjusticebooks.org/guide-for -selecting-anti-bias-childrens-books.

National Associations

Alliance for Childhood supports networks committed to improving the lives of children through play. www.allianceforchildhood.org

Inclusive Schools Network provides web-based resources related to inclusive educational practices. https://inclusiveschools.org /category/resources/early-childhood

National Association for Bilingual Education (NABE) advocates for educational equity and educational excellence for bilingual /multilingual students. www.nabe.org

National Association for the Education of Young Children (NAEYC) advocates for high-quality early childhood practices. NAEYC.org

National Institute for Early Education is a research organization dedicated to inform policy that supports high-quality early childhood education. https://nieer.org

National Institute for Play is a nonprofit corporation dedicated to highlighting the benefits of play. www.nifplay.org

Riddles and Tongue Twisters in Spanish and English

Neuro-Nita. 2002. *¿Podrás con los trabalenguas? ¿Y con las adivinanzas?* San Ángel: Editorial y Distribuidora Leo.

Songs and Games in Spanish and English

123 Andrés provides Spanish and English songs for young dual language learners. www.123andres.com

Ella Jenkins with Smithsonian Folkway Recordings has a collection of multicultural children's songs in various languages. www.ellajenkins.com

Guia Infantil includes traditional play games of children from many cultures. www.guiainfantil.com

José-Luis Orozco is a bilingual educator, children's author, and recording artist. His website provides numerous resources for dual language classrooms. https://joseluisorozco.com/main/index.html

Songs from ROCK (Region One Curriculum Kit), by Carol Perkins. This CD has a collection of thematic songs and songs based on traditional children's fairy tales in English and Spanish.

Songs for Teaching has a collection of multicultural songs for children. www.songsforteaching.com

Student Names

Institute of Education Sciences. 2016. *Getting It Right: Reference Guides for Registering Students with Non-English Names.* Report. https://ies.ed.gov/ncee/edlabs/projects/project.asp?projectID=4533.

My Name, My Identity Campaign was created by the Santa Clara County Office of Education and its Multilingual & Humanities Education Department. www.mynamemyidentity.org

Teaching with Equity

Friedman, S., & A. Mwenelupembe, eds. 2020. *Each and Every Child: Teaching Preschool with an Equity Lens.* Washington, DC: NAEYC.

Hansel, L., ed. 2019. Embracing Anti-Bias Education [issue cluster topic]. *Young Children* 74 (5).

Total Physical Response

Total Physical Response: www.theteachertoolkit.com/index.php/tool/total-physical-response-tpr.

Video and directions to implement Total Physical Response: www.theteachertoolkit.com/index.php/tool/total-physical-response-tpr

subtractive language environments:
Environments in which DLLs have few opportunities to speak, listen, read, and write in their home language. In these settings, English is the predominant language of instruction and the language reflected in most instructional materials and environmental print.

total physical response (TPR):
A specific ESL strategy designed to provide children with gestures that will help them learn vocabulary in a second language. (Asher 1966).

translanguage: DLLs alternate language codes for meaningful purposes—to communicate without concerns about adhering to a prescribed language.

translanguaging: May involve alternation of languages, as well as use of other resources (gestures, visual resources, languages, etc.) to convey meaning: "I ♥ you. You are my favorite *tío* [uncle]."

translingual play: Involves DLLs flexibly using their languages during play in meaningful interactions without correction or constraints of language choice.

two-way dual language: Programs that include speakers of two language groups (e.g., Spanish-dominant children and English-dominant children participate in balanced numbers) who are learning content in two languages.

zone of proximal development: A concept developed by Lev Vygotsky that explains the range of ability between what children can do alone versus what they can do with assistance from a more knowledgeable other. Social interaction is a critical part of this process. Buddy reading is an example because stronger readers assist peers with the reading process by modeling reading strategies, asking questions, or explaining the process.

About the Authors

Iliana Alanís, PhD, a native of South Texas, is a professor of early childhood and elementary education in the department of interdisciplinary learning and teaching at the University of Texas–San Antonio. She taught children in bilingual first- and second-grade classrooms while earning a master's degree in curriculum and instruction with a concentration in bilingual education from the University of Texas–Pan American.

She completed her PhD at the University of Texas at Austin in Curriculum and Instruction with specializations in Multilingual Studies and Educational Psychology. As a university faculty member, she engages teacher candidates and practicing teachers for their work in culturally and linguistically diverse classrooms with a primary focus on the rights of young children to develop their linguistic and cultural identity. In her research, Dr. Alanís uses a sociocultural lens to examine effective pedagogical practices in early childhood, dual language contexts. Dr. Alanís provides professional development for dual language teachers across the country, serves as a board member for various early childhood associations, and advocates for dual language learners and their families.

María G. Arreguín, EdD, is an associate professor of early childhood and elementary education in the department of interdisciplinary learning and teaching at the University of Texas–San Antonio. She earned her doctoral degree in Bilingual Education at the Texas A&M University–Kingsville. Her research on dual language education, early childhood education, dyad learning and dialogue, and critical science pedagogy illuminates the intricacies of cultural and linguistic factors that influence minority children's access to education in early childhood and elementary bilingual settings.

Dr. Arreguín has been involved with the Texas Association for Bilingual Education and the National Association for Bilingual Education in different capacities. In both organizations, she seeks to link educational research and educational policy to target the very issues directly addressed in her scholarly work.

Irasema Salinas-González, EdD, is an associate professor and coordinator of the early care and early childhood studies program at the University of Texas–Rio Grande Valley (UTRGV). During her 29 years in the bilingual and early childhood education fields, she has been a preschool and kindergarten teacher and reading specialist, and has worked with preservice and in-service teachers. She received her MEd in Early Childhood Education from the University of Texas–Pan American and her EdD in Bilingual Education from Texas A&M University–Kingsville. Her work focuses on language and literacy development of young dual language learners through play, the development of cognitive skills of dual language learners through play-based learning, and creating engaging classroom environments for young dual language learners.

Dr. Salinas-González has served as a board member for Hidalgo County Head Start and UTRGV Early Head Start Child Care Partnership program at the Pharr-San Juan-Alamo school district. During her tenure at UTRGV, she has served as Principal Investigator and Co-Principal Investigator for several early childhood education grants, giving her the opportunity to collaborate with the Kellogg Foundation as well as the US Department of Health and Human Services, Administration for Children and Families, Children's Learning Institute. She is currently coordinating a grant with the Texas Education Agency. She has also served as an educational consultant to early childhood education centers and public school districts, where she advocates for developmentally, culturally, and linguistically appropriate practices for young dual language learners.

Index

Page numbers followed by an "*f*" refer to figures, "*t*" refer to tables.

family involvement in creating, 36–38
functional print, 42–44
materials and spaces, 39–41
playful learning, 59

Codeswitching, 18, 26, 64, 91

Cognitive academic language proficiency, 27

Color-coding labels, 42–43

Colored salt, writing with, 41

Communicating with families, means of, 7–8

Community
environmental print, 41–42
funds of knowledge, 37
learning about, 6
materials from the, 48, 109
outreach, 7–8

Comprehensive input, 76, 76*f*

Consistency, establishing, 44–46

Contextualized learning example, 101–110

Conversational language. *See* Language of informal communication; Reciprocal conversations

Cooperative play, 55

Countries of origin, 5

Cross-cultural perspectives
goals of dual language programs, 24
interactional language, 29

Cross-language spaces, 18, 19

Culture and cultural issues
cultural capital of children and families, 4, 6, 7, 36–38
incorporating discussions of culture, 14
interactional language, 29
interdisciplinary biliteracy approach, 109–110
story content, 80–81

_____

D

Dance, 80

Demographics, 5–6

Deportation fear, 9

Dialogic reading, 81, 104

Displays, classroom, 39–40

Dominant language
bilingual continuum, 90
identification of, 14
language inventory, 69*t*

Dramatic play, 51–53, 56, 57*f*

Drawing, 38, 66–67, 96, 105

Dual language learner labels, 4

_____

E

Emergent bilinguals, 4, 61–62

Emotional well-being of children, 44, 109

English as a second language (ESL)
classrooms, 76, 95
total physical response, 79–80

English language learner (ELL) label, 4

Environmental print, 41–42, 44, 48

ESL. *See* English as a second language (ESL)

Essential support provision, 44–46

Exploration and discovery, 62, 64, 66, 72, 109

Expressive language skills, 26, 29, 90

Extension activities for children with disabilities, 19

_____

F

Family
assessment process, 88–89
building with familial boxes, 56
developing relationships with, 7–10
family-teacher conferences, 89
interdisciplinary biliteracy approach, 109–110
involvement in creating the classroom environment, 36–38, 48
learning about, 6–7
literacy stationery, 55
partnerships with, 3
sharing development progress with, 89

Family-generated alphabet, 37–38, 39

Functional print, 42–44, 47

Funds of knowledge, 37

_____

G

Gesture, use of, 53, 79, 90

Goals of dual language programs, 24, 87, 89

Group discussion, 64, 67

Group learning centers, 41

H

Hands-on types of assessment, 96

Home language
access to instruction in, 75–76
assessment strategies, 97
during play, 59
questions involving, 10–11
support services, 97
survey, 88, 89*t*
validating, 8
See also Bilingualism and biliteracy development

I

IDEA (Individuals with Disabilities Education Act), 46

Identifying the dominant language, 14

Identity validation, 8

IEP (individualized Education Plan), 57

IFSP (Individualized Family Service Plan), 57

Imaginative language, 29

Immigrants
languages spoken at home, 7

Inclusive play, 57–58

Individualized Education Plan (IEP), 57

Individualized Family Service Plan (IFSP), 57

Individuals with Disabilities Education Act (IDEA), 46

Integrated lesson example, 101–110, 115

Interactional language, 28–29, 28*t*

Interactive read-alouds, 67

Interactive word walls, 43–44

Interdisciplinary biliteracy approach, 64–68, 65*f*, 103–110, 112–113

Interest centers. *See* Learning centers

Interpersonal communication skills, 27

Interpreters, use of, 6–7, 89, 97

K

Kinesthetic teaching strategies, 79

Knowledge transfer, 16–17, 18

L

Labels
dual language learners, 4
interactive labels, 42–43
learning enhancement, 19
using labels from home, 39

Language arts. *See* Bilingualism and biliteracy development

Language development, key aspects of, 20*t*

Language dominance. *See* Dominant language

Language environments, 14–16

Language experience approach, 64

Language input strategies, 27–29

Language inventory, 69, 69*t*

Language minority, 4

Language of communication, 29

Language of informal communication, 21, 27

Language of instruction, 26, 27, 29, 70, 73

Language of learning, 26–27, 29, 73

Language practices in local dual language schools, 25

Language proficiency, 21

Language-rich experiences, 80–82

Language transfer, 16, 17, 18, 18*t*

Languages spoken, 5–6, 5*f*, 7

Learning centers, 40–41, 106–108, 112–113

Least restrictive environment, 46

Letter searches, 43

Limited English proficient (LEP) label, 4

Linguistically accommodated instruction, 21

Linguistic or language scaffolding, 54–55, 63

Linguistic repertoire, 17, 17*t*

Listening skills. *See* Oracy

Literacy materials, 41

Literacy spaces for play, 58

Logos, 41–42

M

Magnifying words and objects, 44

Manipulatives. *See* Objects and manipulatives

Materials, classroom, 39–41, 46–47, 58

Meaning
biliteracy development, 66
focus on, 18–20
language of learning, 26, 29, 73
manipulatives, use of, 78
social language, 94
translingual partner-based activities, 68
word walls, 70

Metalinguistic awareness, 17

Mix-pair-share strategy, 80

Modeling
interactional language, 28
partner-based learning, 82, 83
play, 58
transitions and routines, 105–106

Monolingual teachers, 30

Morning message, 102–103, 104f

Movement, 79–80

Multimodal experiences, 46, 68–69, 77–80

Multiple label acquisition, 16, 17

Multiple languages, assessment in, 91

Music, 80

N

NAEYC (National Association for the Education of Young Children), 4, 108–109

Name pronunciation, 8

National Academies of Sciences, Engineering, and Medicine, 91

National Association for the Education of Young Children (NAEYC), 4, 108–109

National Head Start Act (2007), 4

Non-dual language learners, 84

Note-taking as assessment tool, 92

O

Object-name association, 19

Objects and manipulatives, 78

Observation
assessment tools, 92, 93t, 94
onlooker play, 54, 55

One-way dual language programs, 23–24

Onlooker play, 54, 55

Oracy
biliteracy development, 62–63, 64–66, 71, 71t, 72
mixing of languages, 73
partner-based learning, 82–83
reciprocal conversations, 81, 88–89

Oral language visibility, 109

Outreach, family and community, 7–8

P

Parallel play, 54

Partner-based learning
biliteracy development, 68–70, 70t
mix-pair-share, 80
non-dual language learners, 84
oracy development, 82–83

Peer interaction. See Partner-based learning

Photographs, 37, 38, 93–94

Pictures, 77

Play, 51–56, 57f, 106

Plyler v. Doe, 6

Professional development for teachers, 30

Pronunciation of names, 8

Props for play, 56, 57f

Purposeful assessment, 92–93

Purposeful planning and cross-language spaces, 19

Q

Quantity of language exposure, 27

R

Read-alouds
biliteracy development, 67–68, 71
integrated lesson example, 104–105

Reading
biliteracy development, 63–64, 72
culturally relevant stories, 80–81
integrated lesson example, 104–105

Receptive language skills, 62, 71, 72, 90

Reciprocal conversations, 81, 88–89

Refugee families, 6

Relationship building, 109

Discover NAEYC!

The National Association for the Education of Young Children (NAEYC) promotes high-quality early learning for all young children, birth through age 8, by connecting early childhood practice, policy, and research. We advance a diverse, dynamic early childhood profession and support all who care for, educate, and work on behalf of young children.

NAEYC members have access to award-winning publications, professional development, networking opportunities, professional liability insurance, and an array of members-only discounts.

Accreditation—NAEYC.org/accreditation

Across the country, **NAEYC Accreditation of Early Learning Programs** and **NAEYC Accreditation of Early Childhood Higher Education Programs** set the industry standards for quality in early childhood education. These systems use research-based standards to recognize excellence in the field of early childhood education.

Advocacy and Public Policy—NAEYC.org/policy

NAEYC is a leader in promoting and advocating for policies at the local, state, and federal levels that expand opportunities for all children to have equitable access to high-quality early learning. NAEYC is also dedicated to promoting policies that value early childhood educators and support their excellence.

Global Engagement—NAEYC.org/global

NAEYC's Global Engagement department works with governments and other large-scale systems to create guidelines to support early learning, as well as early childhood professionals throughout the world.

Professional Learning—NAEYC.org/ecp

NAEYC provides face-to-face training, technology-based learning, and Accreditation workshops—all leading to improvements in the knowledge, skills, and practices of early childhood professionals.

Publications and Resources —NAEYC.org/publications

NAEYC publishes some of the most valued resources for early childhood professionals, including award-winning books, *Teaching Young Children* magazine, and *Young Children*, the association's peer-reviewed journal. NAEYC publications focus on developmentally appropriate practice and enable members to stay up to date on current research and emerging trends, with information they can apply directly to their classroom practice.

Signature Events—NAEYC.org/events

NAEYC hosts three of the most important and well-attended annual events for educators, students, administrators, and advocates in the early learning community.

NAEYC's Annual Conference is the world's largest gathering of early childhood professionals.

NAEYC's Professional Learning Institute is the premier professional development conference for early childhood trainers, faculty members, researchers, systems administrators, and other professionals.

The **NAEYC Public Policy Forum** provides members with resources, training, and networking opportunities to build advocacy skills and relationships with policymakers on Capitol Hill.

NAEYC.org/membership

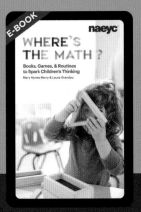
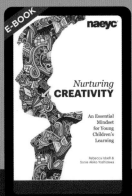

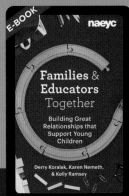

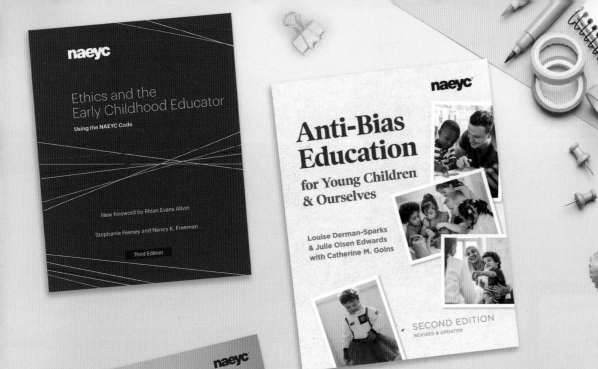

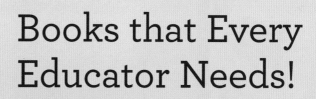

Books that Every Educator Needs!

NAEYC.org/shop